Internet Governance at the Point of No Return

Rolf H. Weber

Internet Governance at the Point of No Return

Author: Prof. Dr. Rolf H. Weber
Publisher: EIZ Publishing
Production, Set & Distribution: buch & netz (buchundnetz.com)
ISBN:
978-3-03805-360-6 (Print – Hardcover)
978-3-03805-392-7 (PDF)
978-3-03805-393-4 (ePub)
978-3-03805-394-1 (mobi/Kindle)
DOI: https://doi.org/10.36862/eiz-360
Version: 0.78 – 20210413

Published with support by the Swiss National Science Foundation (SNF).

This work is available in print and various digital formats in **OpenAccess**. Additional information is available at: https://buchundnetz.com/werke/internet-governance-at-the-point-of-no-return/.

Preface

Internet governance is on the move. For the last 20 years, governments (international organizations and national bodies), businesses and non-governmental entities, civil society as well as academia have attempted to develop a normative framework for the Internet world. The globalization of data exchanges and of digital transactions calls for innovative principles of governance and for the transformation of traditional concepts in order to adequately reflect the expectations of all involved Internet actors. As a result, there is a need to re-think the social, cultural, economic, technical, and legal spheres of the new environment.

At the beginning, Internet governance mainly had a technological foundation. In the meantime, experience has shown that political challenges gained importance over the previous "technical" issues. As a consequence, it is imperative to embed the applicable regulations into a normative Internet governance ecosystem. Accordingly, the rule-making power over the mechanics of the Internet warrants a broader assessment.

During the last two decades, the author was involved in the development of Internet governance concepts in legal and in interdisciplinary research projects as well as in his capacity as expert for international organizations and as member of global associations in this field. In 2017, some key results and insights from this work were published as re-prints in a book ("Normative Movements in Internet Governance and Cyberlaw", Bern 2017). Since then new developments have occurred and merit to be analyzed; therefore, an update of and a conceptual "upgrade" on the manifold fresh ideas seems timely.

The present publication aims at giving an overview of the most relevant legal principles that play a substantive role in the Internet governance context as well as at designing possible rule-making pillars for an adequate normative Internet environment. Irrespective of some political tensions, the chances are fair that Internet governance has come to the *point of no return* which calls on academia to contribute its share in shaping the ecosystem.

Zurich, January 2021   Rolf H. Weber

Contents

Bibliography

All weblinks have last been checked on 31 January 2021. Many additional references to specific topics are cited in the footnotes.

A

Abbott/Snidal, 2000. Kenneth W. Abbott/Duncan Snidal, Hard and Soft Law in International Governance, International Organization 54 (2000), 421-456

Almeida/Getschko/Afonso, 2015. Virgílio Almeida/Demi Getschko/Carlos Afonso, The Origin and Evolution of Multistakeholder Models, IEEE Internet Computing 19 (2015), 74-79

Amstutz, 2011. Marc Amstutz, Mechanisms of Evolution for a Law of the Future, in: Müller/Zouridis/Frishman/Kistemaker (eds.), The Law of the Future and the Future of Law, Oslo 2011, 395-405

Antonova, 2008. Slavka Antonova, Powershape of Internet Governance, Saarbrücken 2008

B

Baldwin/Cave/Lodge, 2012. Robert Baldwin/Martin Cave/Martin Lodge, Understanding Regulation: Theory, Strategy, and Practice, 2nd ed., New York 2012

Basedow, 2008. Jürgen Basedow, The State's Private Law and the Economy: Commercial Law as an Amalgam of Public and Private Rule-Making, American Journal of Comparative Law 56 (2008), 703-721

Bekkers/Martinelli, 2012. Rudi Bekkers/Arianna Martinelli, Knowledge positions in high-tech markets: Trajectories, standards, strategies and true innovators, Technological Forecasting and Social Change 79 (2012), 1192-1216

Belli, 2021. Luca Belli (ed.), CyberBRICS. Cybersecurity Regulations in the BRICS Countries, Cham 2021

Benhabib, 2006. Seyla Benhabib, Another Cosmopolitanism, Oxford 2006

Benkler, 2011. Yochai Benkler, Network Theory: Networks of Power, Degrees of Freedom, International Journal of Communication 5 (2011), 721-755

Benkler, 2006. Yochai Benkler, The Wealth of Networks: How Social Production Transforms Markets and Freedom, New Haven/London 2006

Berman, 2007. Paul Schiff Berman, Global Legal Pluralism, Southern California Law Review 80 (2007), 1155-1237

Bernstein/Cashore, 2007. Steven Bernstein/Benjamin Cashore, Can non-state global governance be legitimate? An analytical framework, Regulation & Governance 1 (2007), 347-371

Biegel, 2001. Stuart Biegel, Beyond Our Control?, Confronting the Limits of Our Legal System in the Age of Cyberspace, Cambridge MA 2001

Black, 2008. Julia Black, Constructing and contesting legitimacy and accountability in polycentric regulatory regimes, Regulation & Governance 2 (2008), 137-164

Blind/Gauch, 2008. Knut Blind/Stephan Gauch, Trends in ICT standards: the relationship between European standardisation bodies and standards consortia, Telecommunications Policy 32 (2008), 503-513

Blind/Gauch/Hawkins, 2010. Knut Blind/Stephan Gauch/Richard Hawkins, How stakeholders view the impacts of international ICT standards, Telecommunications Policy 34 (2010), 162-174

Braithwaite/Drahos, 2000. John Braithwaite/Peter Drahos, Global Business Regulation, Cambridge 2000

Braman, 2020. Sandra Braman, The Irony of Internet Governance Research: Metagovernance as Context, in: DeNardis/Cogburn/Levinson/Musiani (eds.), Researching Internet Governance – Methods, Frameworks, Futures, Cambridge MA/London 2020, 21-57

Brousseau/Marzouki/Méadel, 2012. Eric Brousseau/Meryem Marzouki/Cécile Méadel (eds.), Governance, Regulations and Powers on the Internet, Cambridge 2012

Brown/Marsden, 2013. Ian Brown/Christopher T. Marsden, Regulating Code: Good Governance and Better Regulation in the Information Age, Cambridge MA/London 2013

Brummer, 2014. Chris Brummer, Minilateralism, Cambridge 2014

Butler, 2020. Jay Butler, The Corporate Keepers of International Law, American Journal of International Law 114 (2020), 189-220

Buzatu, 2015. Anne-Marie Buzatu, Multi-Stakeholder Approaches to Governance: Challenges and Opportunities, DCAR Horizon Working Paper, Vol. 8, Geneva 2015

Bygrave/Bing, 2009. Lee A. Bygrave/Jon Bing (eds.), Internet Governance: Infrastructure and Institutions, Oxford 2009

C

Caney, 2006. Simon Caney, Justice Beyond Border: A Global Political Theory, Oxford 2006

Cartwright, 2020. Madison Cartwright, Internationalising state power through the internet: Google, Huawei and geopolitical struggle, Internet Policy Review 9/3 (2020), https://doi.org/10.14763/2020.3.1494

Chik, 2010. Warren B. Chik, "Customary Internet-ional Law": Creating a Body of Customary Law for Cyberspace. Part I: Developing Rules for Transitioning Custom into Law, Computer Law & Security Review 26 (2010), 3-22

Chin, 2020. Yik Chan Chin, Internet governance in China: The network governance approach, in: Wang/Pavlićević (eds.), Social Relations and Political Development in China: Change and Continuity in a "New Era", London 2020, 134-153

Chin/Changfeng, 2018. Yik Chan Chin/Chen Changfeng, Internet Governance: Exploration of Power Relationship, January 2018, https://ssrn.com/abstract=3107239

Clark, 2005. Ian Clark, Legitimacy in International Society, New York 2005

Cogburn, 2020. Derrick L. Cogburn, Big Data Analytics and Text Mining in Internet Governance Research: Computed Analysis of Transcripts from 12 Years of the Internet Governance Forum, in: DeNardis/Cogburn/Levinson/Musiani (eds.), Researching Internet Governance – Methods, Frameworks, Futures, Cambridge MA/London 2020, 185-211

Cohen, 2020. Julie E. Cohen, Networks, Standards, and Network-and-Standard-Based Governance, in: Werbach (ed.), After the Digital Tornado – Networks, Algorithms, Humanity, Cambridge 2020, 57-80

Cotterrell, 2009. Roger Cotterrell, Spectres of Transnationalism: Changing Terrains of Sociology of Law, Journal of Law and Society 36 (2009), 481-500

D

Dany, 2008. Charlotte Dany, Civil Society Participation under Most Favorable Conditions: Assessing the Deliberative Quality of the WSIS, in: Steffek/Kissling/Nanz (eds.), Civil Society Participation in European and Global Governance, Paul Grave 2008, 53-70

De Búrca/Keohane/Sabel, 2014. Gráinne de Búrca/Robert O. Keohane/Charles F. Sabel, Global Experimentalist Governance, British Journal of Political Science 40 (2014), 477-486

Delvenne/Parotte, 2019. Pierre Delvenne/Céline Parotte, Breaking the myth of neutrality: Technology Assessment has politics, Technology Assessment as politics, Technological Forecasting and Social Change 139 (2019), 64-72

DeNardis, 2020a. Laura DeNardis, Introduction: Internet Governance as an Object of Research Inquiry, in: DeNardis/Cogburn/Levinson/Musiani (eds.), Researching Internet Governance – Methods, Frameworks, Futures, Cambridge MA/London 2020, 1-20

DeNardis, 2020b. Laura DeNardis, The Internet in Everything – Freedom and Security in a World with No Switch Off, New Haven/London 2020

DeNardis, 2014. Laura DeNardis, The Global War for Internet Governance, New Haven/London 2014

DeNardis, 2011. Laura DeNardis, Opening Standards: The Global Politics of Interoperability, Cambridge MA 2011

DeNardis, 2009. Laura DeNardis, Protocol Politics: The Globalization of Internet Governance, Cambridge MA 2009

De Vey Mestdagh/Rijgersberg, 2006. Kees de Vey Mestagh/Rudolf W. Rijgersberg, Rethinking Accountability in Cyberspace: A New Perspective on ICANN, International Review of Law, Computers & Technology 21 (2006), 29-40

Doria, 2013. Avri Doria, Use [and Abuse] of Multistakeholderism in the Internet, in: Radu/Chenou/Weber (eds.), The Evolution of Global Internet Governance, Principles and Policies in the Making, Zürich 2013, 115-138

E

Easterbrook, 1996. Frank H. Easterbrook, Cyberspace and the Law of the Horse, The University of Chicago Legal Forum 1996, 207-216

Epstein/Katzenbach/Musiani, 2016. Dmitry Epstein/Christian Katzenbach/Francesca Musiani, Doing internet governance: How science and technology studies inform the study of internet governance, Internet Policy Review 5/3 (2016), 3-14

Ewert/Kaufmann/Maggetti, 2020. Christian Ewert/Céline Kaufmann/Martino Maggetti, Linking democratic anchorage and regulatory authority: the case of internet regulators, Regulation & Governance 14 (2020), 184-202

F

Ferguson/Morris, 1994. Charles H. Ferguson/Charles R. Morris, Computer Wars, New York 1994

Foucault, 1978/79. Michel Foucault, Naissance de la biopolitique: Cours au Collège de France (1978-1979), Paris 2004

Franck, 1995. Thomas M. Franck, Fairness in International Law and Institutions, Oxford 1995

Friedmann, 1974. Wolfgang Friedmann, The Changing Structure of International Law, New York 1974

Fuchs, 2020. Christian Fuchs, Communication and Capitalism: A Critical Theory, London 2020

Fukuyama, 2004. Francis Fukuyama, Governance and the Order in the Twenty First Century, London 2004

G

Gasser/Budish/West, 2015. Urs Gasser/Ryan Budish/Sarah Myers West, Multistakeholder as Governance Groups: Observations from Case Studies, Berkman Center Research Publication No. 2015-1, Cambridge MA 2015

GCSC-Report, 2019. Global Commission on the Stability of Cyberspace, Advancing Cyberstability, Final Report, Berlin (IGF), November 2019

Gleckman, 2018. Harris Gleckman, Multistakeholder Governance and Democracy. A Global Challenge, London 2018

Grotius, 1916. Hugo Grotius, The freedom of the seas or the right which belongs to the Dutch to take part in the East Indian Trade: a dissertation, ed. by James Brown Scott, New York 1916

Guzman/Meyer, 2010. Andrew T. Guzman/Timothy L. Meyer, International Soft Law, Journal of Legal Analysis 2 (2010), 171-225

H

Habermas, 2006. Jürgen Habermas, Does the Constitutionalization of International Law Still Have a Chance?, in: Habermas (ed.), The Divided West, Cambridge 2006, 93-115

Habermas, 1992. Jürgen Habermas, Faktizität und Geltung, Frankfurt 1992

Haggart, 2019. Blayne Haggart, Taking Knowledge Seriously: Toward an International Political Economy Theory of Knowledge Governance, in: Haggart/Henne/Tusikov (eds.), Technology and Control in a Changing World: Understanding Power Structures in the 21st Century, New York 2019, 25-52

Haggart/Tusikov/Scholte, 2021. Blayne Haggart/Natasha Tusikov/Jan Aart Scholte, Power and Authority in Internet Governance, London 2021

Harcourt/Christou/Simpson, 2020. Alison Harcourt/George Christou/Seamus Simpson, Global Standard Setting in Internet Governance, Oxford 2020

Hart, 1997. Herbert L.A. Hart, The Concept of Law, 2nd ed., Oxford 1997

Heald, 2006. David Heald, Varieties of Transparency, in: Hood/Heald (eds.), Transparency – The Key to Better Governance?, Oxford 2006, 25-43

Heintschel von Heinegg, 2013. Wolff Heintschel von Heinegg, Territorial Sovereignty and Neutrality in Cyberspace, International Legal Studies 89 (2013), 123-156

Héritier/Lehmkuhl, 2011. Adrienne Héritier/Dirk Lehmkuhl, New Modes of Governance and Democratic Accountability, Government and Opposition 46 (2011), 126-144

Hobbes, 1651. John Hobbes, Leviathan or the Matter, Forme & Power of a Common-Wealth Ecclestiasticall and Civill, London 1651

Hoffmann/Lazanski/Taylor, 2020. Stacey Hoffmann/Dominique Lazanski/Emily Taylor, Standardising the splinternet: how China's technical standards could fragment the internet, Journal of Cyber Policy 5/2 (2020), 239-264

Hofmann, 2020. Jeannette Hofmann, The Multistakeholder Concept as Narrative: A Discourse Analytical Approach, in: DeNardis/Cogburn/Levinson/Musiani (eds.), Researching Internet Governance – Methods, Frameworks, Futures, Cambridge MA/London 2020, 253-268

Hofmann, 2016. Jeannette Hofmann, Multi-Stakeholderism in Internet Governance: Putting a Fiction into Practice, Journal of Cyber Policy 1 (2016), 29-49

I

Irion, 2009. Kristina Irion, Separated Together: The International Telecommunication Union and Civil Society, International Journal of Communications Law & Policy 13 (2009), 87-105

J

Johnson/Post, 1998. David R. Johnson/David G. Post, The New "Civic Virtue" of the Internet, First Monday 3(1) (1998), http://doi.org/10.5210/fm.v3i1.570

Johnson/Post, 1996. David R. Johnson/David G. Post, Law and Borders – The Rise of Law in Cyberspace, Stanford Law Review 48 (1996), 1367-1402

Jørgensen, 2013. Rikke Frank Jørgensen, Framing the Net. The Internet and Human Rights, Cheltenham 2013

K

Kaufmann, 2020. Christine Kaufmann, Building on OECD Due Diligence Guidance to Promote Coherence, in: Business & Human Rights Resource Center, Towards EU Mandatory Due Diligence Legislation, eu20.de-Report, November 2020, 77-79

Kaufmann, 2018. Christine Kaufmann, The Covenants and Financial Crises, in: Möckli/Keller (eds.), The Human Rights Covenants at 50, Their Past, Present, and Future, Oxford 2018, 303-333

Kaufmann/Weber, 2010. Christine Kaufmann/Rolf H. Weber, The Role of Transparency in Financial Regulation, Journal of International Economic Law 13 (2010), 779-797

Kaul/Grunberg/Stern, 1999. Inge Kaul/Isabelle Grunberg/Marc A. Stern (eds.), Global Public Goods: International Cooperation in the 21st Century, Oxford 1999

Keck/Sikkink, 1999. Margaret E. Keck/Kathryn Sikkink, Transnational advocacy networks in international and regional politics, International Social Science Journal 51 (1999), 89-101

Kerr/Musiani/Pohle, 2019. Aphra Kerr/Francesca Musiani/Julia Pohle, Communication and internet policy: a critical rights-based history and future, Internet Policy Review 8/1 (2019), doi: 10.14763/2019.1.1395

Kettemann, 2020. Matthias C. Kettemann, The Normative Order of the Internet, Oxford 2020

Kettemann, 2014. Matthias C. Kettemann, The Common Interest in the Protection of the Internet: An International Perspective, in: Benedek et al. (eds.), The Common Interest in International Law, Antwerp 2014, 167-184

Kettemann/Paulus, 2020. Matthias C. Kettemann/Alexandra Paulus, Ein Update für das Internet – Reform der globalen digitalen Zusammenarbeit 2021, sef: Global Governance Spotlight 4/ 2020, 1-4

Kish, 1973. John F. Kish, The Law of International Spaces, Leiden 1973

Kleinwächter, 2021. Wolfgang Kleinwächter, Internet Governance Outlook 2021: Digital Cacaphony in a Splintering Cyberspace, CircleID of 8 January 2021, http://www.circleid.com/posts/20210108-internet-governance-outlook-2021-digital-cacaphony/

Kleinwächter, 2011. Wolfgang Kleinwächter, A new Generation of Regulatory Frameworks: The Multistakeholder Internet Governance Model, in: Sethe et al. (eds.), Kommunikation, Festschrift für Rolf H. Weber, Bern 2011, 559-580

Kleinwächter/Kettemann/Senges/Schweiger, 2020. Wolfgang Kleinwächter/Matthias C. Kettemann/Max Senges/Jörg Schweiger, Cross-Pollination in Cyberspace and the Internet Governance "Spaghetti-Ball": How to Design a Global Mechanism for Digital Cooperation?, CircleID of 26 April 2020, http://www.circleid.com/posts/20200426-cross-pollination-in-cyberspace-internet-governance-spaghetti-ball/

Koh, 2006. Harold H. Koh, Why Transnational Law Matters, Penn State International Law Review 24 (2006), 745-753

Koskenniemi, 2017. Martti Koskenniemi, International Law as "Global Governance", in: Desautels-Stein/Tomlins (eds.), Searching for Contemporary Legal Thought, Cambridge 2017, 199-218

Koskenniemi, 2009a. Martti Koskenniemi, From Apology to Utopia: The Structure of International Legal Argument, 3rd print, Cambridge 2009, 562-573

Koskenniemi, 2009b. Martti Koskenniemi, The Politics of International Law – 20 Years Later, European Journal of International Law 20 (2009), 7-19

Krisch, 2014. Nico Krisch, The Decay of Consent: International Law in an Age of Global Public Goods, American Journal of International Law 108 (2014), 1-40

Kulesza, 2016. Joanna Kulesza, Due Diligence in International Law, Leiden/Boston 2016

Kulesza, 2012. Joanna Kulesza, International Internet Law, London/New York 2012

Kulesza/Weber, 2021. Joanna Kulesza/Rolf H. Weber, Protecting the Internet with International Law, Computer Law & Security Review 40 (2021) 105531, 1–12

Kulesza/Weber, 2017. Joanna Kulesza/Rolf H. Weber, Protecting the Public Core of the Internet, Delhi 2017, https://cyberstability.org/research/briefing-and-memos-of-the-research-advisory-group

Kurbalija, 2016. Jovan Kurbalija, State Responsibility in Digital Space, Swiss Review of International and European Law 26 (2016), 307-325

L

Lanier, 2013. Jaron Lanier, Who owns the future?, London 2013

Lazanski, 2019. Dominique Lazanski, Governance in international technical standards-making: a tripartite model, Journal of Cyber Policy 4/3 (2019), 362-379

Lee/Sohn, 2018. Won S. Lee/So Y. Sohn, Effects of standardisation on the evolution of information and communications technology, Technological Forecasting and Social Change 132 (2018), 308-317

Lessig, 2008. Lawrence Lessig, Remix: Making art and commerce thrive in the hybrid economy, London 2008

Lessig, 2006. Lawrence Lessig, CODE Version 2.0, New York 2006

Lessig, 2004. Lawrence Lessig, Free culture: how big media use technology and the law to lock down culture and control creativity, New York 2004

Lessig, 2001. Lawrence Lessig, The Future of Ideas, New York 2001

Lessig, 1999a. Lawrence Lessig, Code and Other Laws of Cyberspace, New York 1999

Lessig, 1999b. Lawrence Lessig, The Law of the Horse: What Cyberlaw Might Teach, Harvard Law Review 113 (1999), 501-549

Levinson, 2020. Nanette S. Levinson, Internet Governance Research and Methods: Internet Governance Learning, in: DeNardis/Cogburn/Levinson/Musiani (eds.), Researching Internet Governance – Methods, Frameworks, Futures, Cambridge MA/London 2020, 269-294

Locke, 1689. John Locke, Two Treaties of Government, published anonymously, London 1689

Luhmann, 1997. Niklas Luhmann, Die Gesellschaft der Gesellschaft, 2 Bde, Frankfurt 1997

Luhmann, 1993. Niklas Luhmann, Das Recht der Gesellschaft, Frankfurt 1993

Luhmann, 1975. Niklas Luhmann, Legitimation durch Verfahren, 2. Aufl. Darmstadt/Neuwied 1975

Lundqvist, 2017. Björn Lundqvist, Standardization for the Digital Economy: The Issue of Interoperability and Access Under Competition Law, The Antitrust Bulletin 62 (2017), 710-725

M

Mahler, 2019. Tobias Mahler, Generic Top-Level Domains: A Study of Transnational Private Regulation, Cheltenham/Northampton 2019

Mahler, 2014. Tobias Mahler, A gTLD-right? Conceptual challenges in the expanding internet domain namespace, International Journal of Law and Information Technology 22 (2014), 27-48

Malcolm, 2008. Jeremy Malcolm, Multi-Stakeholder Governance and the Internet Governance Forum, Perth 2008

Mantelero, 2018. Alessandro Mantelero, AI and Big Data: A Blueprint for a Human Rights, Social and Ethical Impact Assessment, Computer Law & Security Review 34/4 (2018), 754-772

Marsden, 2020. Christopher T. Marsden, The Regulated End of Internet Law, and the Return to Computer and Information Law?, in: Werbach (ed.), After the Digital Tornado – Networks, Algorithms, Humanity, Cambridge 2020, 35-57

Mayer-Schönberger, 2008. Viktor Mayer-Schönberger, Demystifying Lessig, Wisconsin Law Review 2008, 713-746

Mitchell, 1998. Ronald D. Mitchell, Sources of Transparency: Information Systems in International Regimes, International Studies Quarterly 42 (1998), 109-130

Möldner, 2019. Mirka Möldner, Accountability of International Organizations and Transnational Corporations – A Comparative Analysis, Baden-Baden 2019

Mueller, 2017. Milton L. Mueller, Will the Internet Fragment? Sovereignty, Globalization and Cyberspace, Oxford 2017

Mueller, 2010. Milton L. Mueller, Networks and States. The Global Politics of Internet Governance, Cambridge MA 2010

Mueller, 2002. Milton L. Mueller, Ruling the Root: Internet Governance and the Taming of Cyberspace, Cambridge MA 2002

Mueller/Badiei, 2020. Milton L. Mueller/Farzaneh Badiei, Inventing Internet Governance: The Historical Trajectory of the Phenomenon and the Field, in: DeNardis/Cogburn/Levinson/Musiani (eds.), Researching Internet Governance – Methods, Frameworks, Futures, Cambridge MA/London 2020, 59-83

Mueller/Badiei, 2019. Milton L. Mueller/Farzaneh Badiei, Requiem for a Dream: On Advancing Human Rights via Internet Architecture, Policy & Internet 11/1 (2019), 61-83

Murray, 2012. Andrew D. Murray, Information Technology Law: The Law and Society, Oxford 2012

Murray, 2007. Andrew D. Murray, The Regulation of Cyberspace: Control in the Online Environment, Milton Park 2007

Musiani, 2013. Francesca Musiani, Nains sans géants, Architecture décentralisée et services Internet, Paris 2013

N

Negroponte, 1995. Nicholas Negroponte, Being Digital, New York 1995

O

Ost/van de Kerchove, 2002. François Ost/Michel van de Kerchove, De la pyramide au réseau? Pour une théorie dialectique du droit, Bruxelles 2002

Owen, 2016. Taylor Owen, Disruptive Power – The Crisis of the State in the Digital Age, Oxford 2015

P

Padovani/Santaniello, 2018. Claudia Padovani/Mauro Santaniello, Digital constitutionalism: Fundamental rights and power limitation in the Internet eco-system, International Communication Gazette 80 (2018), 295-301

Palfrey/Gasser, 2012. John Palfrey/Urs Gasser, Interop: The Promise and Perils of Highly Interconnected Systems, New York 2012

Pauwelyn, 2011. Joost Pauwelyn, The Rise and Challenges of "Informal" International Law-Making in: Müller/Zouridis/Frishman/Kistemaker (eds.), The Law of the Future and the Future of Law, Oslo 2011, 125-141

Plato, ed. 1942. Plato, in: Louise Ropes Loomis (ed.), The Five Great Dialogues: Apology, Phaedo, Crito, Symposium, Republic, New York 1942

Pogge, 1994. Thomas Pogge, Cosmopolitanism and Sovereignty, in: Brown (ed.), Political Restructuring in Europe: Ethical Perspectives, London 1994, 85-118

Post, 1991. Robert Post, Law and the Order of Culture, Berkeley/Los Angeles/Oxford 1991

Q

R

Radu, 2019. Roxana Radu, Negotiating Internet Governance, Oxford 2019

Raustiala, 2017. Kal Raustiala, Governing the Internet, The American Journal of International Law 110 (2017), 491-503

Raustiala, 2002. Kal Raustiala, The Architecture of International Cooperation: Transgovernmental Networks and the Future of International Law, Virginia Journal of International Law 43 (2002), 1-92

Raymond/DeNardis, 2015. Mark Raymond/Laura DeNardis, Multistakeholderism: anatomy of an inchoate global institution, International Theory 7 (2015), 572-616

Rawls, 1971. John Rawls, Theory of Justice, Cambridge 1971

Redeker/Gill/Gasser, 2018. Dennis Redeker/Lex Gill/Urs Gasser, Towards digital constitutionalism? Mapping attempts to craft an Internet Bill of Rights, International Communication Gazette 80 (2018), 302-319

Reed, 2012. Chris Reed, Making Laws for Cyberspace, Oxford 2012

Reidenberg, 1998. Joel R. Reidenberg, Lex Informatica: The Formulation of Information Policy Rules Through Technology, Texas Law Review 76 (1998), 553-593

Rioux, 2013. Michèle Rioux, Competing Institutional Trajectories for Global Regulation – Internet in a Fragmented World, in: Radu/Chenou/Weber (eds.), The Evolution of Global Internet Governance – Principles and Policies in the Making, Zürich 2013, 37-55

Rodrik, 2010. Dani Rodrik, The Globalization Paradox: Democracy and the Future of the World Economy, New York 2010.

Rousseau, 1754/62. Jean-Jacques Rousseau, The Social Contract and Discourses by Jean-Jacques Rousseau, translated with an Introduction by George D. H. Cole, London/Toronto 1923, http://oll.libertyfund.org/title/cole-the-social-contract-and-discourses

Ruggie, 1975. John Gerard Ruggie, Reconstituting the Global Public Domain – Issues, Actors and Practices, European Journal of International Relations 10 (2004), 499-531

Ryga, 1995. Barbara M. Ryga, Cyberporn: Contemplating the First Amendment in Cyberspace, Seton Hall Constitutional Law Journal 6 (1995), 221-253

S

Sand, 2009. Inger Johanne Sand, Law in a Global Society of Differentiation and Change, in: Callies/Fischer-Lescano/Wielsch/Zumbansen (eds.), Soziologische Jurisprudenz, Festschrift für Gunther Teubner zum 65. Geburtstag, Berlin 2009, 871-886

Sassen, 2008. Saskia Sassen, Territory, Authority, Rights: From Medieval to Global Assemblages, 2nd ed. Princeton 2008

Sayle, 2000. Amber Jene Sayle, Net Nation and the Digital Revolution: Regulation of Offensive Material for a New Community, Wisconsin International Law Journal 18 (2000), 257-285

Scholte, 2004. Jan Aart Scholte, Civil society and democratically accountable global governance, Government and Opposition 39 (2004), 211-233

Segura-Serrano, 2006. Antonio Segura-Serrano, Internet Regulation and the Role of International Law, in: Max Planck Yearbook of United Nations Law, Vol. 10, The Hague 2006, 191-272

Senn, 2015. Myriam Senn, Transnationalität im Recht als Herausforderung, Zeitschrift für Schweizerisches Recht 134 I (2015), 493-512

Senn, 2011. Myriam Senn, Non-State Regulatory Regimes. Understanding Institutional Transformation, Heidelberg et al. 2011

Shaffer, 2012. Gregory Shaffer, Transnational Legal Process and State Change, Law & Social Inquiry 37 (2012), 229-264

Slaughter, 2004. Anne-Marie Slaughter, A New World Order, Princeton/Oxford 2004

Smit/Bright, 2020. Lise Smit/Claire Bright, Human Rights and Environmental Due Diligence as a Standard of Care, in: Business & Human Rights Resource Center, Towards EU Mandatory Due Diligence Legislation, eu20.de-Report, November 2020, 51-54

Spindler/Thorun, 2016. Gerald Spindler/Christian Thorun, Die Rolle der Ko-Regulierung in der Informationsgesellschaft – Handlungsempfehlung für eine digitale Ordnungspolitik, Multi-Media und Recht, Beilage zu 6/2016, 1-28

Stoll, 2008. Peter-Tobias Stoll, Global Public Goods – The Governance Dimension, in: Rittberger/Nettesheim (eds.), Authority in the Global Political Economy, New York 2008, 116-136

Suzor, 2019. Nicolas P. Suzor, Lawless: The Secret Rules That Govern Our Digital Lives (and Why We Need New Digital Constitutions That Protect Our Rights), Cambridge 2019

T

Tambini/Leonardi/Marsden, 2008. Damian Tambini/Danilo Leonardi/Chris Marsden, Codifying Cyberspace: Communications self-regulation in the age of Internet convergence, London 2008

Teubner, 2012. Gunther Teubner, Constitutional Fragments: Societal Constitutionalism and Globalisation, Oxford 2012

Teubner, 1989. Gunther Teubner, Recht als autopoietisches System, Frankfurt 1989

Thelisson, 2012. Eva Thelisson, Un Etat Mondial via Internet?, Puteaux 2012

U

Uerpmann-Wittzack, 2010. Robert Uerpmann-Wittzack, Principles of International Internet Law, German Law Journal 11 (2010), 1245-1263

V

Van Huijstee, 2012. Mariette van Huijstee, Multi-Stakeholder Initiatives: A Strategic Guide for Civil Society Organizations, Amsterdam 2012, https://papers.ssrn.com/sol3/papers.cfm?abstract_id=2117933

Voelsen, 2021. Daniel Voelsen, Internet aus dem Weltraum, SWP-Studie, Berlin 2021

Voelsen, 2019. Daniel Voelsen, Risse im Fundament des Internets. Die Zukunft der Netzinfrastruktur und die globale Internet Governance, SWP-Studie, Berlin 2019

W

Waz/Weiser, 2012. Joe Waz/Philip J. Weiser, Internet Governance: The Role of Multistakeholder Organizations, Journal of Telecommunications & High Technological Law 10 (2012), 331-350

Weber, 2021a. Rolf H. Weber, Duty of Co-operation as New Cybergovernance Concept, IT Jusletter (Weblaw) of 25 February 2021

Weber, 2021b. Rolf H. Weber, "Infinite Space" – International Legal Concepts as Path to Internet Integrity, (forthcoming)

Weber, 2020a. Rolf H. Weber, A Legal Lense into Internet Governance, in: DeNardis/Cogburn/Levinson/Musiani (eds.), Researching Internet Governance – Methods, Frameworks, Futures, Cambridge MA/London 2020, 105-121

Weber, 2020b. Rolf H. Weber, Cybersecurity in International Law, in: Asian Academy of International Law (ed.), 2019 Colloquium on International Law, Synergy and Security, Hong Kong 2020, 280-313

Weber, 2018. Rolf H. Weber, "Rose is a rose is a rose is a rose" – what about code and law?, Computer Law & Security Review 34 (2018), 701-706

Weber, 2016a. Rolf H. Weber, Elements of a Legal Framework for Cyberspace, Swiss Review of International and European Law 26 (2016), 195-215

Weber, 2016b. Rolf H. Weber, Legal foundations of multistakeholder decision-making, Zeitschrift für Schweizerisches Recht 135 I (2016), 247-267

Weber, 2015. Rolf H. Weber, New "Cosmopolitically" Founded Concepts for the Cyberworld, in: Biaggini/Diggelmann/Kaufmann (eds.), Polis und Kosmopolis, Festschrift für Daniel Thürer, Zürich/St.Gallen 2015, 779-786

Weber, 2014a. Rolf H. Weber, Realizing a New Global Cyberspace Framework, Zürich 2014

Weber, 2014b. Rolf H. Weber, Legal Interoperability as a Tool for Combating Fragmentation, Global Commission for Internet Governance, Paper Series No. 4, Waterloo (CA), December 2014

Weber, 2013. Rolf H. Weber, Visions of Political Power: Treaty Making and Multistakeholder Understanding, in: Radu/Chenou/Weber (eds.), The Evolution of Global Internet Governance, Principles and Policies in the Making, Zurich 2013, 95-113

Weber, 2012. Rolf H. Weber, Future Design of Cyberspace Law, Journal of Politics and Law 5 (2012), 1-14

Weber, 2011. Rolf H. Weber, Accountability in the Internet of Things, Computer Law & Security Review 27 (2011), 133-138

Weber, 2009. Rolf H. Weber, Shaping Internet Governance: Regulatory Challenges, Zürich 2009

Weber, 2008. Rolf H. Weber, Transparency and the Governance of the Internet, Computer Law & Security Review 24 (2008), 342-348

Weber, 2002. Rolf H. Weber, Regulatory Models for the Online World, Zürich 2002

Weber/Gunnarson, 2012. Rolf H. Weber/R. Shawn Gunnarson, A Constitutional Solution for Internet Governance, The Columbia Science and Technology Law Review XIV (2012), 1-71

Weber/Menoud, 2008. Rolf H. Weber/Valérie Menoud, The Information Society and the Digital Divide – Legal Strategies to Finance Global Access, Zürich 2008

Weber/Weber, 2009. Rolf H. Weber/Romana Weber, Social Contract for the Internet Community? Historical and Philosophical Theories as Basis for the Inclusion of Civil Society in Internet Governance, SCRIPT-ed 6 (2009), 90-105

Weitzenboeck, 2014. Emily M. Weitzenboeck, Hybrid net: the regulatory framework of ICANN and the DNS, International Journal of Law and Information Technology 22 (2014), 49-73

Weitzenboeck, 2012. Emily M. Weitzenboeck, A Legal Framework for Emerging Business Models – Dynamic Networks as Collaborative Contracts, Cheltenham/Northampton 2012

Weyrauch/Winzen, 2020, David Weyrauch/Thomas Winzen, Internet Fragmentation, Political Structuring, and Organizational Concentration in Transnational Engineering Networks, Global Policy 2020, doi:10.1111/1758-5899.12873

Wolfrum, 2010. Rüdiger Wolfrum, Co-operation, International Law of, in: Wolfrum (ed.), Max Planck Encyclopedia of Public International Law, Oxford, December 2010 (update online)

X

Y

Z

Zingales/Radu, 2016. Nicolo Zingales/Roxana Radu, In search for the holy grail: a principled approach to multistakeholder governance in internet policy-making, in: Prince/Kuipers/ Lindseth/Rosina (eds.), Digital Democracy in a Globalized World, Cheltenham/Northampton 2017, 53-76

Zittrain, 2008. Jonathan Zittrain, The Regulation of the Internet and How to Stop It, New York 2008

Zuboff, 2019. Soshana Zuboff, The Age of Surveillance Capitalism, New York 2019

Abbreviations

APC	Association for Progressive Communications
ARPANET	Advanced Research Projects Agency Network
Art.	Article
CA	Certificate Authority
ccTLD	Country Code Top-Level Domain
CERT	Computer Emergency Response Team
CESCR	Committee on Social, Economic and Cultural Rights
CIR	Critical Internet Resource
COM	(European) Commission Document
CSIRT	Computer Security Incident Response Team
DDoS	Distributed Denial of Service
DNS	Domain Name System
DNSSEC	Domain Name System Security Extensions
Doc.	Document
DoC	Department of Commerce (United States)
DPI	Deep Packet Inspection
DRM	Digital Rights Management
DSL	Digital Subscriber Line
ed./eds.	Editor/editors
EFF	Electronic Frontier Foundation
e.g.	For example
ETNO	European Telecommunications Network Operators' Association
EU	European Union
EuroDig	European Dialogue on Internet Governance
FCC	Federal Communications Commission
Fn.	Footnote
FTP File	File Transfer Protocol
GATS	General Agreement on Trade in Services
GATT	General Agreement on Tariffs and Trade
GNI	Global Network Initiative
gTLD	Generic Top-Level Domain
HTML	Hypertext Markup Language
IAB	Internet Architecture Board
IANA	Internet Assigned Numbers Authority
ICANN	Internet Corporation for Assigned Names and Numbers
ICC	International Chamber of Commerce
ICCPR	International Covenant on Civil and Political Rights

ICESCR	International Covenant on Economic, Social, and Cultural Rights
ICJS	Statute of the International Court of Justice
ICT	Information and Communication Technologies
i.e.	That is ("id est" in Latin)
IEEE	Institute of Electrical and Electronics Engineers
IESG	Internet Engineering Steering Group
IETF	Internet Engineering Task Force
IGF	Internet Governance Forum
IGO	Inter-Governmental Organization
IP	Internet Protocol
IPR	Intellectual Property Rights
IPsec	Internet Protocol Security
IPv4	Internet Protocol Version 4
IPv6	Internet Protocol Version 6
IOSCO	International Organization of Securities Commissions
ISO	International Organisation for Standardisation
ISOC	Internet Society
ISP	Internet Service Provider
IT	Information Technology
ITR	International Telecommunication Regulations
ITU	International Telecommunication Union
IXP	Internet Exchange Point
JPEG	Joint Photographic Experts Group
LAN	Local Area Network
LIR	Local Internet Registries
MA	Massachusetts
NGO	Nongovernmental Organization
NIR	National Internet Registry
No.	Number
NSA	National Security Agency
NSI	Network Solution Inc.
NTIA	National Telecommunications and Information Administration
OECD	Organization for Economic Cooperation and Development
OSI	Open Systems Interconnection
p./pp.	Page/pages
P2P	Peer-to-Peer
P3P	Platform for Privacy Preferences
para./paras.	Paragraph/paragraphs
PET	Privacy Enhancing Technologies
QoS	Quality of Service

RfC	Request for Comments
RFID	Radio-Frequency Identification
RIPE NCC	Réseaux IP Européens-Network Coordination Centre
RIR	Regional Internet Registry
SMTP	Simple Mail Transfer Protocol
SNA	Systems Network Architecture
TBT	Technical Barriers to Trade
TCP	Transmission Control Protocol
TCP/IP	Transmission Control Protocol/Internet Protocol
TLD	Top-Level Domain
TLS	Transport Layer Security
TRIPS	Trade Related Aspects of Intellectual Property Rights
TTP	Trusted Third Party
UDHR	Universal Declaration of Human Rights
UDRP	Uniform Domain-Name Dispute-Resolution Policy
UN	United Nations
UNCITRAL	United Nations Commission on International Trade Law
UNCTAD	United Nations Conference on Trade and Development
UNDP	United Nations Development Programme
UNESCO	United Nations Educational, Scientific and Cultural Organization
URL	Uniform Resource Locator
US	United States
VoIP	Voice over Internet Protocol
Vol.	Volume
W3C	World Wide Web Consortium
WCIT	World Conference on International Telecommunications
WGEC	Working Group on Enhanced Cooperation
WGIG	Working Group on Internet Governance
WIPO	World Intellectual Property Organization
WSIS	World Summit on the Information Society
WTO	World Trade Organization
WWW	World Wide Web

I.   Introduction

In February 1996, the late John Parry Barlow published the famous *"Declaration of the Independence of Cyberspace"* containing many emphatic pronouncements such as: "I declare the global social space we are building to be naturally independent of the tyrannies you seek to impose on us. You have no moral right to rule us nor do you possess any methods of enforcement we have true reason to fear. Cyberspace does not lie within your borders."[1]

Subsequently, scholars have taken up Barlow's approach and have assigned attributes of independence to the new "province". Terms like "net nation" for the participants in cyberspace were created[2] and traditional laws were disregarded due to the fact that they have been conceived in and for a world of atoms rather than bits. As an example the following quote is remarkable: "The Internet is a place where anyone is welcome, regardless of gender, age, race, or association. ... Since there is no regulatory body policing the Internet, the extent to which an individual is capable of speaking without restriction is an enigma."[3]

Is such kind of assessment of cyberspace still realistic? The answer to this question will be negative from most persons of whatever discipline, geographic region or cultural background. Cyberspace is not fully independent but at least partially influenced by States' interferences; the traditional legal environment developed into the new global infrastructure. Governments are indeed concerned about the "legalization" of cyberspace.

Within the last 30 years the Internet's evolution has been enormous.[4] Starting as a communication system to be used for military purposes, the everywhere and anytime accessible Internet, encompassing social, cultural, and legal facets, has become essential to daily life at least in the developed countries' world. In the light of the technological progresses made a number of questions arise: How will data exchange networks look like in 10 or 15 years? What role

---

[1]   See <https://projects.eff.org/de/cyberspace-independence>; the Declaration could recently celebrate its 25th anniversary.

[2]   See *Sayle*, 2000, 281 et seq.; in parallel, civil society more and more moved to a status of being digital (*Negroponte*, 1995, *passim*).

[3]   *Ryga*, 1995, 223; for a critical assessment of this opinion see already *Weber*, 2002, 26, and *Biegel*, 2001, *passim*.

[4]   The following text is based on *Weber*, 2016a, 196 et seq.

will such networks play in the future society and (how) will they change existing social structures? Opinions on these subjects are diverse, ranging from an improvement of the society's current state by for example supporting less developed countries up to a dismal future scenario of a monitored world controlled by technology.

In the context of the search for the ideal social order a number of theoretical models have been developed in the past, among others the so-called utopia and dystopia.

(i)   Utopia (literally translated as "no-place") refers to a non-existent society, place or state being viewed as considerably better than the contemporary society. Having been coined by Sir Thomas Morus as title of his well-known book "Utopia" (1516) the term utopia describes an imaginary place where social, political and moral aspects are considered to be perfect.

(ii) In contrast, dystopia (literally translated as "not-good place"), linked to dehumanization, totalitarian governments or other declines in society, reflects the situation of an undesirable community. Many subgenres of fiction deal with dystopian societies for calling attention to real-world issues such as corruption in politics, environmental pollution, religious wars or unethical behavior.

Transferring these different scenarios to the Internet ecosystem the question arises whether the future Internet leaves some room for a society between "no-place" and "not-good place".

Looking from a socio-political perspective, society cannot exist without a minimal legal order, at least – as developed by Jean-Jacques Rousseau[5] – in the form of a "social contract". But any legal order also has social impacts, i.e. concepts and designs need to be transformed into reality. Such kind of perception was not obvious in the past: (i) Plato understood his democracy proposal in "Republic" as utopian idea.[6] (ii) Thomas Morus envisaged in his novel "Utopia" a paradise on a fictional island in the Atlantic Ocean on which an ideal society could exist.[7] (iii) In the 19th century, many social movements in Europe searched for various forms of utopian environments. The non-existing society as reflecting the definition of utopia converges into an ideal society in these theoretical models.[8]

During the last fifty years efforts have been undertaken to better incorporate Utopian projects into the structure of legislative or regulatory (national and

---

[5]   Rousseau, 1754/62; for further details see Weber, 2009, 74 et seq.

[6]   Plato, ed. 1942, Republic.

[7]   Thomas Morus, Utopia, London 1516.

[8]   Weber, 2014a, 107.

international) regimes. Initially qualified as "framework of utopia",[9] more recently autonomous cultural arrangements were assessed through the lens "From Apology to Utopia" by way of outlining the international legal order's descriptive and normative concerns.[10] Next to the Utopian projects some fifty years ago the voices pointing to dystopian societies became louder, for example in "Nineteen Eighty-Four" showing a totalitarian invasive super State[11] or in "Fahrenheit 451" addressing the burning of books to create apathy and disinterest in the general public.[12]

Nevertheless, even with a higher degree of concretization, "utopia" and "dystopia" are not ideal concepts for the design of an appropriate future Internet framework since it is difficult to identify sufficiently clear contours. In addition, it seems quite impossible to draw on normative or structural elements, aiming at future developments from these concepts. Moreover, a large decision-making discretion is left to the potential rulers in charge. As a consequence, the design of a normative environment encompassing the realization of key substantive principles appears to be unavoidable.

Originally, the term "Internet governance" was used to describe the administration and design of the technologies that keep the Internet operational and allow the enactment of policies around these technologies. Even if such an approach does not constitute an ideal taxonomy for the manifold aspects of structure, coordination, and control mechanisms, some important functions are usually described as follows:[13] (i) administration of critical Internet resources such as names and numbers; (ii) establishment of Internet technical standards (e.g. protocols, routing, authentication); (iii) coordination of access and interconnection; (iv) cybersecurity governance; (v) policy-making roles of private information intermediaries; and (vi) architecture-based intellectual property rights enforcement.

Over time, it has become increasingly clear that the technical design and coordination of the Internet is a part of public policy. Subsequent challenges

---

[9] *Robert Nozick*, Anarchy, State and Utopia, New York 1974.
[10] *Koskenniemi*, 2009a, 562 et seq.
[11] *George Orwell*, Nineteen Eighty-Four, London 1949.
[12] *Ray Bradbury*, Fahrenheit 451, New York 1953.
[13] For a recent description of Internet governance see *DeNardis*, 2020a, 3; for further elements see *Weber*, 2014a, 4 (with references); *Eric Brousseau/Meryem Marzouki*, Internet governance: old issues, new framings, uncertain implications, in: Brousseau/Marzouki/Méadel, 2012, 371 et seq.; *Bygrave/Bing*, 2009, *passim*; for a good overview outlining the historical trajectory of Internet Governance see *Mueller/Badiei*, 2020, 59 et seq.

concern the multiple levels of involved bodies (from the individual to the inter-organizational), the increasing role of non-state actors, the multilayered interactions (cross-border, cross-cultural, transnational), and the complex regulatory questions.[14] Furthermore, the Internet as the most important global "infrastructure" impacts the Nation-state jurisdiction and (in connection with the upholding of its integrity) the national security concerns. In such an environment, the notion of Internet governance has been widened to cybergovernance.[15]

This book firstly attempts to shed light on the potential technological developments caused by alternative network infrastructures and the interconnectedness between the different networks. Based on this analysis the yardsticks of an adequate normative framework are addressed; in particular, regulatory theories that allow overcoming the weaknesses of previous approaches are sketched in more detail. As a result, the elements of a new normative design will be analyzed. Thereby, three research questions can be identified at the horizon: (i) Are adequate theories of regulation (addressing traditional rationales and social/technological changes) available? (ii) How should an appropriate legal framework for cyberspace be designed? (iii) Which normative principles are to be realized in cyberspace?

Thereafter, the substantive principles governing the Internet ecosystem (legitimacy, participation, transparency, accountability) merit to be further elaborated. Finally and most importantly, the foundations of cybergovernance and the available international legal concepts designing its outreach are discussed and thoroughly assessed. Thereby, a "holistic approach" will be applied making the realities of the fast-changing environment in an interconnected world compatible with the implementation of sound political strategies.

---

[14]   See also *Levinson*, 2020, 285.

[15]   For further details see *Weber*, 2021a, nos. 1 et seq.

II. Technological Developments and Standardization

A. Expansion of New Infrastructures

The Internet of these days has already been established some decades ago. In the meantime, technological developments are allowing the transport of more data on manifold infrastructures, mainly due to the means of digital communication channels and the new distributed ledger technology (DLT).[16] Notwithstanding this situation, the capacity of networks partly becomes limited as the debates about network neutrality are showing; furthermore, new Internet protocols are needed around the globe (i.e. in all countries irrespective of the state of economic development) as the ongoing movement from IPv4 to IPv6 is showing.[17]

Apart from the traditional fixed line and the expanding mobile networks, new technological inventions are attempting to facilitate the transmission of data. The aim of these attempts is to provide reasonably fast, high-quality connections to almost everyone at whatever location. Usually, the chosen approach is a top-down model not based on the familiar terrestrial technologies.

The following new developments, mentioned as not limited number of examples, are particularly noteworthy:

- The US firm OneWeb planned to launch 648 small, relatively simple satellites into low orbits of 1200 km altitude providing latency similar to that offered by a fixed line connection. Since a single satellite would be able to provide backhaul to some villages at the time, local operators should be able to afford phone masts or Internet base-stations in order to pro-

---

[16] The following text is based on *Weber*, 2016a, 198/99.

[17] See *Iljitsch van Beijnum*, With the Americas running out of IPv4, it's official: The Internet is full, Ars Technica, 6 December 2014, <https://arstechnica.com/information-technology/2014/06/with-the-americas-running-out-of-ipv4-its-official-the-internet-is-full/>.
In November 2020, about 43% of the US and Swiss users accessed Google on the basis of the IPv6 protocol, see <https://www.google.com/intl/en/ipv6/statistics.html#tab=per-country-ipv6-adoption>.

vide the capillary distribution.[18] After OneWeb filed for relief under Chapter 11 of the US-Bankruptcy Code in March 2020,[19] a UK government consortium acquired the firm and assured to complete the construction of a global satellite constellation.[20]

– The firm SpaceX of Elon Musk, the co-founder of Paypal and now the owner of Tesla (producer of electric cars), intends to place about 4'000 satellites at a similar altitude of the orbit (project called "Starlink"). However, the satellites should be more sophisticated insofar as they are not only providing Internet access to the unconnected but would also serve other markets.[21]

– A subsidiary of Amazon, namely "Kuiper", is developing a project being similar to "Starlink": More than 3'000 satellites should be available for Internet services around the world; the US Federal Communications Commission (FCC) granted the respective license for the US territory in July 2020.[22]

– Google has started to experiment with drones, i.e., with high-altitude balloons: The "Project Loon"[23] consists in the attempt to grid the Earth with a swarm of thousands of helium-filled balloons; each balloon should carry a solar-powered wireless transmitter and be capable of relaying traffic from other balloons.[24] In July 2018, Project Loon spun out into a separate company.[25]

---

[18] *Rolfe Winkler*, Greg Wyler's OneWeb Satellite-Internet Company Secures Funding, The Wall Street Journal, 14 January 2015, <http://www.wsj.com/articles/greg-wylers-oneweb-satellite-internet-company-secures-funding-1421278832>.

[19] See <https://www.oneweb.world/media-center/oneweb-files-for-chapter-11-restructuring-to-execute-sale-process>.

[20] *Jonathan O'Callaghan*, U.K. Government Wins Controversial Bid for Bankrupt Mega Constellation Firm OneWeb, Forbes, 3 July 2020, <https://www.forbes.com/sites/jonathanocallaghan/2020/07/03/uk-government-wins-controversial-bid-for-bankrupt-mega-constellation-firm-oneweb/?sh=37f3f13a5b9d>; see also *Voelsen*, 2021, 15.

[21] *Dave Majumdar*, Why the Time Seems Right for a Space-Based Internet Service, MIT Technology Review, 27 January 2015, <https://www.technologyreview.com/2015/01/27/169490/why-the-time-seems-right-for-a-space-based-internet-service/>; for further details see *Voelsen*, 2021, 11 and 15.

[22] Amazon Company News, Amazon Receives FCC Approval for Project Kuiper Satellite Constellation, 30 July 2020, <https://www.aboutamazon.com/news/company-news/amazon-receives-fcc-approval-for-project-kuiper-satellite-constellation>; see also *Voelsen*, 2021, 15.

[23] See <https://www.google.com/loon/>.

[24] *Tom Simonite*, Alphabet's Stratospheric Loon Balloons to Start Serving Internet to Indonesia, MIT Technology Review, 28 October 2015, <https://www.technologyreview.com/2015/10/28/109668/alphabets-stratospheric-loon-balloons-to-start-serving-internet-to-indonesia/>.

[25] *Jillian D'Onfro*, Alphabet spins drone and internet balloon projects into independent companies, CNBC, 11 July 2018, <https://www.cnbc.com/2018/07/11/alphabet-projects-wing-and-loon-spin-out-into-separate-companies.html>.

- Facebook's "Project Aquila" which originated in its "Connectivity Lab" consisted in the attempt to plug specific gaps in the existing infrastructure since satellites are inherently inefficient (by flying over places where no one lives, such as oceans); special solar-powered drones were intended to provide basic access to a small number of sites free for users of the Internet.org app.[26] In June 2018, Facebook announced that it would stop this project and would not design or build its own aircraft any longer.[27]

- Pursuing a similar approach as Facebook, "HAPSMobile", a joint venture of SoftBank and AeroVironment, has developed a solar-powered drone that is designed to deliver 5G connectivity.[28] As announced in April 2019, HAPSMobile will work together with Project Loon, inter alia, by developing common ground stations for their Internet infrastructure.[29]

For all projects, a regulatory framework will become important; having a considerable impact on many social issues, new technological innovations with disruptive effects can hardly survive without an adequate legal "environment". Political or normative problems could contribute to a crisis of States' structures in the digital era and lead to disruptive power.[30]

Very recently it has become known that a new technological innovation in the context of the network infrastructure has the potential to gradually replace the well-known Transport Control Protocol (TCP) having been the transport layer for data packages on the Internet for more than forty years. The protocol "Quic", developed and then submitted by Google, is seen as valuable alternative basis protocol for the Internet by the Internet Engineering Task Force (IETF), the main standardization organization in this field. The further progress of this protocol and its acceptability by the concerned actors remains to be observed.

---

[26] See <https://info.internet.org/en/story/connectivity-lab/> and *Tom Simonite*, Facebook's Drones Will Battle Google's Balloons to Spread Internet Access, MIT Technology Review, 27 March 2014, <https://www.technologyreview.com/2014/03/27/173531/facebooks-drones-will-battle-googles-balloons-to-spread-internet-access/>.

[27] Yael Maguire, High altitude connectivity: The next chapter, Facebook Engineering, 27 June 2018, <https://engineering.fb.com/2018/06/27/connectivity/high-altitude-connectivity-the-next-chapter/>; *Adam Satariano*, Facebook Halts Aquila, Its Internet Drone Project, The New York Times, 27 June 2018, <https://www.nytimes.com/2018/06/27/technology/facebook-drone-internet.html>.

[28] See <https://www.hapsmobile.com/en/>.

[29] *Jon Russell*, Internet connectivity projects unite as Alphabet spinout Loon grabs $125M from SoftBank's HAPSMobile, Tech Crunch, 25 April 2019, <https://techcrunch.com/2019/04/24/alphabet-spinout-loon-grabs-125m-from-softbank/>.

[30] See *Owen*, 2015, 22-47.

B.   Technological Standardization

New technologies in the hardware and in the software context require inter-operability to the widest feasible extent; therefore, standardization of the developed goods (products and services) as well as of the procedures appears to be imperative for establishing an adequate design appropriately embracing the future network infrastructures.[31] Standardization is usually achieved on the basis of deliverables (in the form of methodologies for assessment or checklists) developed by expert groups and subsequently accepted by the members of the concerned community; if widely acknowledged, standards are suitable to demonstrate compliance with regulatory requirements.[32]

1.   Origins of and Organizations for Standardization

Technological standardization has its origin in the electrotechnical field. The development of international standards started with the International Elec-trotechnical Commission (IEC), established in 1906, and the International Fed-eration of the National Standardizing Associations (ISA) of 1926; two decades later, in 1946, the International Organisation for Standardisation (ISO)[33] came into being, replacing the ISA and the United Nations Standards Coordinating Committee (UNSCC).

Aiming at promoting the "international coordination and unification of indus-trial standards" the ISO has already published about 20'000 International Stan-dards covering most aspects of technology and manufacturing with the excep-tion of the fields of electricity and electronic transmission in which the standards are set by the IEC and the International Telecommunication Union (ITU).[34] Today, the ISO, the ITU and the IEC are considered to be the standards setters worldwide and collaborate under the banner of the World Standards Cooperation (WSC).

Apart from the WSC, particularly in the Internet field the Internet Engineering Task Force (IETF), a "large open international community of network design-ers, operators, vendors, and researchers"[35] produces technical documents

---

[31]   This sub-chapter is based on *Weber*, 2016a, 212-214.
[32]   See also *Lazanski*, 2019, 362 et seq.
[33]   See <https://www.iso.org/about-us.html>.
[34]   *Senn*, 2011, 171.
[35]   See <https://www.ietf.org/about/>.

influencing the way Internet users design, use, and manage the Internet. The IETF with its technical "Requests for Comments" (RfC) is the main driver of the standardization of the Internet protocols[36] as in place and applied today.[37]

Originally founded in 1865 to promote co-operation among international telegraphy networks,[38] the ITU combines members from 193 countries and almost 800 private-sector entities and academic institutions. The ITU members attempt to achieve the definition and adoption of (voluntary) standards through consensus agreements between the national delegations representing their country's economic groups; accordingly, the developed standards reflect a broad range of international experience and knowledge. The most important legal instrument governing network infrastructures are the International Telecommunications Regulations (ITR); during the World Conference on International Telecommunications (WCIT) in December 2012 (Dubai) the members negotiated an update of the ITR with provisions related to the Internet but diverging political concepts about several issues (for example the interpretation of the term "security") caused the result that an unanimous adoption of the new rules failed.[39]

2.   Benefits of Standardization

Many advantages exist and can be achieved if participants of a technology or infrastructure are using harmonized standards based on common technical understandings for the development of goods or in the context of services delivery. Even though often invisible, standards are of importance for raising the levels of the products' quality, efficiency and interchangeability by providing a framework for the assessment of their conformity.[40]

Being instrumental in facilitating international trade, standards make things work. Once the majority of a particular industry's goods or services are in line with the standards set, a state of industry-wide standardization exists.[41] Standards for goods and services also work as strategic tools for businesses that thereby can reduce their costs by minimizing errors and faulty/unsuccessful developments.

---

[36]   For a general discussion see *Mueller*, 2002, and *DeNardis*, 2009.

[37]   See IETF, About IETF, <http://www.ietf.org/about/>.

[38]   See <https://www.itu.int/en/about/Pages/default.aspx>.

[39]   For further details see *Weber*, 2013, 99 et seq.

[40]   *Senn*, 2011, 173; see also *Blind/Gauch/Hawkins*, 2010, 173 et seq.

[41]   *Senn*, 2011, 173, for the Internet standardization see also *Mueller*, 2002, and *DeNardis*, 2009.

Besides that, standards of different natures can constitute a contribution for companies in the efforts to open up new markets, to level the playing field for developing countries and to support the development of a free and fair global trade.[42] For these reasons, particularly the ISO remains very active in the preparation of new standards facilitating the cross-border co-operation (lately for example in the field of security in information technology).

3. Challenges of Standardization

Particularly in the field of ICT, standardization may – as some authors argue – also "restrict" technological change and development. According to them, standardization can block the introduction of new, non-standard technologies through lock-in effects and lay down path-dependency for future products and technological trajectories.[43] Therefore, standardization potentially contains the disadvantage of hindering timely updates to meet technological change and thus concentrate technologies around the given standard.[44]

Whether standardization leads to such effects and, if yes, to what extent, builds the contents of various research projects which cannot be discussed in detail hereinafter.[45] However, it is worth mentioning that this research has been criticized for overemphasizing the lock-in effects based on insufficient empirical evidence; in addition, studies have proven that standardization can also have the effect of fostering technological diversity.[46]

Furthermore, standardization by non-governmental organizations could cause the problem that the respective bodies exercise an unchecked authority,[47] that a possibility for regulatory arbitrage is available[48] and that the public

---

[42] See <http://www.iso.org/iso/home/about.htm>.

[43] See *John Seaman*, "China and the New Geopolitics of Technical Standardization", Notes de l'Ifri, January 2020, available at: <https://www.ifri.org/sites/default/files/atoms/files/seaman_china_standardization_2020.pdf>.

[44] *Lee/Sohn*, 2018, 308, with further references.

[45] See also *Blind/Gauch, passim,* and *Bekkers/Martinelli, passim.*

[46] *Lee/Sohn*, 2018, 308 and 316 with further references.

[47] *Cohen*, 2020, 66 et seq. ; very recently, two political scenarios for the implementation of regulations in the satellite communication context have been sketched, namely the model of global oligopolies and the model of regulated competition (see *Voelsen*, 2021 20 et seq.

[48] *Cohen*, 2020, 68 et seq.

accountability is becoming doubtful.[49] However, experience has shown that standards developed by non-state actors and being acknowledged by the concerned community have the potential to achieve a wide-spread acceptance and to design a co-regulatory framework in which governmental agencies also assume some fundamental functions (for example general surveillance).[50]

4. Standardization for New Network Infrastructures

The advantages of a technological standardization are particularly obvious in the development of new network infrastructures.[51] By using (voluntary) standards globally, market access barriers are likely to be removed. In the network infrastructure context, standards are based on a given or developed architecture as the example of the Internet (but also the newer distributed ledger technology) clearly shows. Several elements can design such kind of architecture:[52]

–   The architecture must be robust and open-ended enough in order to enable an extension from a niche into a general-purpose platform.

–   Architectures are usually distributed through "products" (goods and services) using their capabilities.

–   A difficult architectural challenge concerns the tensions between diffusion and control potentially leading to selective open designs.

In the Internet environment, the standardization has been mainly driven from the early-stage uncertainties to a quite stable infrastructure as developed by the IETF; the mentioned community of designers, operators, and researchers produces the technical documents influencing the way of using and managing the Internet. Even if the architecture is decentralized, the standards achieve a high degree of harmonization. Thereby, the originators do not have the force or power of giants but are influential through conviction.[53] Nevertheless, it cannot be overlooked that in recent times technical standards of powerful

---

[49]   *Cohen,* 2020, 73 et seq.; to what extent (political, ethical) "values" can be interpreted into technical standards is subject to an intensive scholarly debate (see *Mueller/Badiei,* 2019, 61 et seq.).

[50]   See *Weber,* 2014a, 23/24.

[51]   A detailed analysis is offered by *Harcourt/Christou/Simpson,* 2020, *passim.*

[52]   See also the more extensive list of *Ferguson/Morris,* 1994, 168/69; to the open standards requirement see *Voelsen,* 2021, 33.

[53]   For more details see *Musiani,* 2013, *passim.*

countries cause the risk of fragmenting the Internet;[54] a similar effect can occur if big private enterprises of a specific country mandatorily impose certain standards.[55]

In view of the global character of network infrastructures (such as in case of the Internet), international standardization has the task to not only provide a level playing field amongst the different offerors of the infrastructure services but also to assure that the important services meet internationally recognized levels of performance and safety. Networks and standards also contribute to the transnational governance[56] and, consequently, to a cosmopolitan regulatory approach.[57]

Standardization helps to realize widely accepted good principles, practices or guidelines in a given area; thereby, standards enshrine the usual behavior of the "reasonable man" (or *"pater familias"* in the Roman law terminology). As a consequence, standardization constitutes an important element in the process of regulating the concerned ecosystem. The more diverging technical characteristics are tied into a standardization framework, the higher is the likelihood of reaching a consensus-oriented and coherent policy environment.

The development of technical standards is usually also concerned with interface issues making different systems interoperable; already for many years, access to and interoperability between networks are topics thoroughly dealt with by competition/antitrust law.[58] Furthermore, standardization can equally contribute to the important legal interoperability of regulatory systems as well as to the harmonization of contractual provisions and terms of services (ToS) in transactional arrangements and for platform businesses. Legal interoperability[59] is a crucial element in the context of a global infrastructure since it helps to overcome an undesired Internet fragmentation.[60]

---

54 The example of China is decribed in detail by *Hoffmann/Lazanski/Taylor*, 2020, 239 et seq.
55 The example of Google and Huawei is described in detail by *Cartwright*, 2020, *passim*.
56 *Cohen*, 2020, 60 et seq.
57 See below Chapter III.D.4.
58 See *Lundqvist*, 2019, 710 et seq.
59 For further details see *Weber*, 2014b, 8 and *Palfrey/Gasser*, 2012, 181 et seq.
60 See below Chapter V.A.3.

III. Foundations of Law and Regulatory Models

A. Law and Regulation as Societal Tools

Notwithstanding the fact that the fast-changing technological and political Internet ecosystem challenges the suitability of traditional regulatory regimes even if the (mentioned) emphatic pronouncements in John Perry Barlow's Declaration of the Independence of Cyberspace (1996) have turned out to be not realistic, law and regulation remain important societal tools. Before discussing available regulatory models, some basic principles of legal theory and the relevant guiding regulatory strategies for Internet governance are worth to be outlined.[61]

1. Structural and Open System

In legal theory, law is seen as a structural system that is composed of an organized or connected group of objects (terms, units, or categories) forming a complex unity. Legal norms are usually expressed in a linguistic manner and are designed to give guidance about the expected behavior.[62] Desirably the addressees, be it the whole society or a concerned part thereof, should take proper note of the contents of law. In principle, legal concepts help support adequate normative reasoning and stabilize societal expectations.[63]

The functions of law crystallize in a system of rules and institutions that underpin civil society, facilitate orderly interaction, and resolve conflicts and disputes arising in spite of the rules.[64] Law can be created through different processes, namely for example by negotiations among the concerned norm addressees (a "social contract", following the concept of Rousseau), by imposition of legal rules by the governing body, or by evolution of self-regulatory mechanisms.[65]

The legal system is not a predetermined construct; moreover, the legal system is embedded in other socially relevant systems. Furthermore, exchange and

---

[61]   The following text (sub-chapters A.1 to A.4) is based on *Weber*, 2020a, 105 et seq.

[62]   *Weber*, 2002, 32.

[63]   *Mahler*, 2014, 27 et seq.; *Weber*, 2014a, 33.

[64]   *Chik*, 2010, 10 et seq.

[65]   *Weber*, 2014a, 33/34; see also *Amstutz*, 2011, 395.

interchange between different social systems make the legal order porous.[66] In the Internet world, the theoretical "models" are mainly influenced by the advances in cybernetics and information theories. In principle, the complexity of any system depends on the inclusion of other organized systems. Since modern societies are differentiated into a plurality of subsystems, a framework of sociological "functionalism" must be developed.

A "meaningful law" in an open system is composed of norms that are perceived as legally binding, thereby inducing the addressees to acknowledge the authority of the rule-making body and to comply with the rules.[67] As a result, law should be able to govern behavior in an appropriate way and to allow people in a community to determine the limits of what can and cannot be done in their collective interests.[68]

2. Relative Autonomy and Flexibility of Law

In view of the rapid technological developments that cause social changes, a flexible legal framework should be realized in order to preserve an open society. This flexibility requires that the normative rules profit from a certain degree of legal autonomy notwithstanding the linkages between different subsystems in society.

The ideal "model" for an open society should be designed in a way that a structural and thorough assessment of the interdependence between normative concepts and other social sciences' perspectives remains possible as outlined hereinafter.

In this context, legal theory scholars have defined criteria for the relative autonomy of law:[69] (1) "Autonomy" means that the law is not equal to and not fully dependent on other social sciences. (2) The word "relative" evidences that exchanges between the law and other social spheres take place in both directions.[70]

The theoretical foundation of the relative autonomy is based on the assumption that other social sciences are not in a position to fully rule out legal flex-

---

[66]   For more details see *Weber*, 2014a, 47.

[67]   *Reed*, 2012, 70-73, 105/06.

[68]   *Weber*, 2014a, 34; for a general discussion of regulatory and governance theories see also *Mahler*, 2019, 72-94, and *Braman*, 2020, 29-33.

[69]   See *Post*, 1991, vii/viii.

[70]   *Weber*, 2002, 36/37.

ibility that is of importance since law needs to be able to react to changing circumstances.[71] In practice, the autonomy model does not directly lead to a clear distinction between law and no law. Generally, however, law may draw on insights from some other fields of discourse while retaining its separate character.

3.   Substance and Change of Law

Legal rules usually contain information having a guiding or even coercive effect on the members of civil society. The legal framework is composed of different instruments:[72]

–   Multilateral or bilateral agreements binding the ratifying countries within the scope of the agreed provisions;

–   Fundamental norms stating substantial values and policies governing the life of the citizens and organizations in a country (usually the constitution);

–   General rules applying to individuals and organizations in the form of a law or an ordinance;

–   Specific judicial or governmental decisions ruling on certain aspects of a legal relation.

To avoid a legal system becoming rigid, mechanisms must be introduced that allow a change of the law in line with the social needs and circumstances. Notwithstanding the fact that the predictability of the law requires a stable structure, the adaptability of legal rules keeps the law intact in case of a relevant social change.[73] The factors of adaption depend on the given "environment"; thereby fundamental principles (such as human rights) are less likely subject to substantive changes than sectorial provisions.

However, before adapting existing laws, lawmakers should consider that legal changes are economically not without cost and do have a social impact because laws are not created in a vacuum. New legal rules could be costly or even risky. Furthermore, addressees of norms may have a limited capacity for attention and new legal rules often impose learning costs on the legal profes-

---

[71]   *Weber*, 2014a, 49/50.

[72]   For a more general overview of the possible legal instruments see *Weber*, 2002, 37/38 and 57 et seq.

[73]   See also *Weber*, 2002, 38.

sion.[74] The development of appropriate guidelines for potential changes of law is particularly important in the Internet field since the technological environment is fast evolving and the global reach of the infrastructure is inherent.

4. Regulatory Strategies and Quality

Traditionally, the legal order was based on a communal, later on a national, normative framework that was complemented by self-regulatory instruments and, since the 19th century, partly by multilateral agreements. This regulatory framework, developed for the real world, is exposed to the challenges if applied to the online world designed by the new information technologies. As a matter of principle, regulatory strategies cannot be implemented without regard to the political landscape that is in the process of being established in the Internet governance field.

An important aspect of Internet governance debates and its normative framework concerns the quality of regulation. Several criteria can improve the desired quality; thereby, the following questions should be taken into account:[75]

- Is the regulatory action supported by legislative authority?

- Does the regime implement an appropriate scheme of accountability?

- Are procedures fair, accessible, and open?

- Is the regulator acting with sufficient expertise?

- Can the regulatory regime be assessed as an efficient system?

In an attempt to improve regulatory quality, the Organization for Economic Cooperation and Development (OECD) issued Guiding Principles for Regulatory Quality and Performance (2005), which encompass an extended scope of relevant aspects that reflect the social and environmental developments:[76]

---

[74] Weber, 2002, 39 with further references.

[75] See Baldwin/Cave/Lodge, 2012, 27-33.

[76] OECD, Guiding Principles for Regulatory Quality and Performance, Paris 2005.

- Adoption of broad programs of regulatory reform that establish key objectives and frameworks for implementation at the political level;

- Systematic assessment of impacts and review of regulations to ensure that the intended objectives are efficiently and effectively reached in a changing and complex economic and social environment;

- Assurance that regulations, regulatory institutions charged with their implementation, and regulatory processes are transparent and non-discriminatory;

- Elimination of unnecessary regulatory barriers to trade and investment by way of continued liberalization and enhancement of market openness throughout the regulatory processes;

- Identification of important linkages with other policy objectives and development of policies to achieve a harmonized regime.

In Internet governance, the appropriateness of these elements remains unchanged, but the approach needs to be widened. As experience has shown, the traditional understanding of political structures as command by a specific body that induces people to execute certain actions – in the sense that people think about what to choose and what to do – should be replaced in the Internet governance context by a more inclusive approach. As a consequence, new theoretical regulatory concepts have been developed, hereinafter shortly described as first and second generation models.

B. First Generation Regulatory Models

Already at the infancy stage of the Internet, academic debates discussing the need for an "Internet Law"[77] and specifically developing theoretical founda-

---

[77] See the partly provocative and interesting debate about the "law of the horse" conducted by *Easterbrook*, 1996, 207–216 and *Lessig*, 1999b, 501–549.

tions for the Internet normative framework have attracted the attention of the legal community.[78] In short, the following theoretical concepts are noteworthy:

1.   Lex Informatica

Even prior to the technology-oriented "code-regulation" approach (Lessig), the concept of a *"lex informatica"* was developed by Joel Reidenberg (1998).[79] Following the idea of the medieval notion of a *"lex mercatoria"*, the *lex informatica* is composed of a set of rules for information flows designed by technology and communication networks that policy-makers must understand.[80] Consequently, information policy rules are formed through technology.

The *lex informatica* concept can be seen as a system of rules analogous to a legal regime.[81] Therefore, it is a "parallel rule system", i.e. a system of technological architectures capable of achieving similar regulatory settlements to that of legal regulations.[82] The *lex informatica* is insofar open as system configurations allow two types of substantive rules, namely immutable policies embedded in technology standards and flexible policies embedded in the technical architecture.[83] Nevertheless, several differences between legal regulations and the *lex informatica* remain to be observed:[84]

---

[78]   The following sub-chapter is based on a more detailed description in *Weber*, 2014a, 53–89.

[79]   *Reidenberg*, 1998, 553 et seq.

[80]   *Reidenberg*, 1998, 555.

[81]   See also *Weber*, 2014a, 61.

[82]   *Reidenberg*, 1998, 565; *Murray*, 2007, 86.

[83]   *Reidenberg*, 1998, 568, 587/88.

[84]   *Reidenberg*, 1998, 569; see also *Weber*, 2014a, 62.

	Legal Regulations	Lex Informatica
Framework	Law	Architectural Standards
Jurisdiction	Physical Territory	Networks
Content	Statutory / Court Expression	Technical Capabilities Customary Practice
Source	State	Technologists
Customized Rules	Contract	Configuration
Customization Process	Low Cost	Off-the-Shelf Configuration
	Moderate Cost Standard Form	Installable Configuration
	High Cost Negotiation	User Choice
Primary Enforcement	Court	Automated, Self-execution

The weakness of the *lex informatica* consists in the lower degree of predictability governing reliable relations between persons. In addition, the setting of the framework for technical solutions, i.e. the democratic legitimacy of the technological "policy-makers", becomes debatable.[85]

2.   Code as Regulator

Among the different approaches to design legal rules in the new technological world the most prominent one refers to the relevance of the "code" as regulatory tool applicable in the Internet. Mainly developed by Lawrence Lessig, this code-related approach deviates from the use of the term "code" as applied by the social and legal scientists such as Niklas Luhmann in the context of the operative closure of a system.[86]

Lessig's concept is based on a complex interrelation between four forces, namely the well-known concepts of "law", "markets", "social norms" and, in addition, "architecture".[87]

---

[85]   Weber, 2014a, 62.

[86]   Luhmann, 1993, 60, 69/70.

[87]   Lessig (1999a, 87) considers architecture as being the most powerful regulator, thereby focusing on the fact that the design of the code materially influences human behavior.

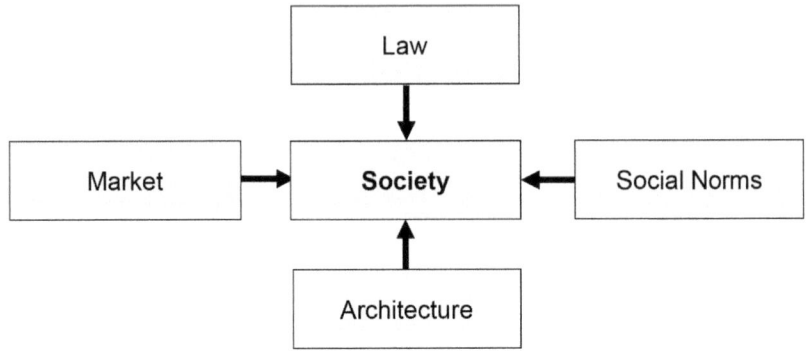

The new element is the architecture combining constraints of physics, nature, and technology.[88] The four factors in Lessig's concept can be translated into the realms of a social order by way of exemplifying their relative importance as follows:[89]

	Architecture – "code"	Economics	Social norms	Law
Enforcement agent	Designers	Market	Peer group	Police, courts
Prior or post facto constraint	Prior – design	During – process	Prior / Post – reputational	Post – sanction
Constraint type	Physical	Economic	Opprobrium	Sanction
Basis of interaction	Structural design	Production and exchange	Social / group	Power
Basis of participation	User	Buyer / seller	Group member	Citizen / subject
Primary institutions	Protocols Engineering institutes	Corporation Enterprise Market	Family Community Church / faith	State Public information

According to Lessig, code "can, and increasingly will, displace law", leading to a world in which "effective regulatory power (shifts) from law to code, from sev-

---

[88] Lessig, 1999a, 87; see also *Mayer-Schönberger*, 2008, 719/20.

[89] The cited table has been developed by *Tambini/Leonardi/Marsden*, 2008, 12; see also *Weber*, 2014a, 56.

erance to software".[90] In respect of who is in control of and responsible for the code, Lessig suggests governments to prevent cyberspace from turning into a commercially controlled place and to take steps to alter or supplement the existing technical architecture for reflecting public policy.[91]

Lessig's approach can be challenged in several ways; mainly the lack of suitability for solving current and future problems in the online world has been criticized.[92] The "code" concept potentially does not comply with individual rights and social values since it is mainly technology-driven; in addition, it does not seem to adequately distinguish between the actual status and the desired outcome but to rely too much on a technological determinism.[93] Furthermore, the perfection of control may be unachievable since at least in theory any code control may be circumvented by another code.[94]

Already in his book "Code 2.0" (2006) Lessig pointed to the risks which can occur depending on the use of the code.[95] More recently, in the blockchain environment the "code" debates gained new relevance. Had Lessig not moved away from this field of research in the meantime, his concerns would probably be even bigger. If "law is code" without any prescription and if everybody is completely free in designing the code for smart contracts, legal developments are exposed to technological misuse.[96] In other words, law must find ways to regulate the code in order to limit its disruptive potential in the hands of irresponsible code designers; the delicate process of aligning legal rules and technical standards does have an impact on the normative system and on the way humans think about law.[97]

3. Formalized Standards and Networks

Assuming that different forms of rules and standards are able to fulfill similar functions as the one previously tied to legal norms in the sense of hard law,

---

[90] *Lessig*, 1999a, 126.
[91] Arguing that code structures rather involve political values than market values, *Lessig* (1999a, 25, 59, 98) wants the most competent body being on top of the pyramid of code (for more details see *Weber*, 2014a, 54-60).
[92] *Weber*, 2014a, 58-60.
[93] *Mayer-Schönberger*, 2008, 736-739.
[94] *Reed*, 2012, 207 et seq.
[95] *Lessig*, 2006, 6.
[96] *Weber*, 2018, 702 et seq., 705.
[97] *Weber*, 2018, 705/06 with further references.

the Internet's regulations can also be conducted through interlinked standards and networks.[98] A prerequisite of this approach consists in the existence of certain justification and persuasion elements in terms of applicable rules.

This approach corresponds to thoughtful ideas developed in legal philosophy by several scholars arguing that the quality of such kind of rule-making reaches at least the same "compliance" level as the traditional legalistic rule-making. In short, the following concepts are noteworthy:[99]

–   Herbert L.A. Hart described the process of formalization and institution-alization or codification of general standards as "secondary norms".[100] Civil society actors can monitor the compliance with rules by applying different instruments.

–   Michel Foucault proclaimed the need for an "art de gouverner"[101] that would allow mirroring the epistemic networks and autonomous self-reg-ulatory organizations in the public interest activities in a better way.

–   Gunther Teubner assessed the weaknesses of international politics and social constitutionalism and expressed the idea that the unity of regula-tory regimes would be significant for the perception of phenomena at dif-ferent (supra-, infra- and trans-state) levels.[102] The law should establish a system for coordination of actions within and between semi-autonomous and societal subsystems.[103]

The subsequent theory of interlinked networks and standards was mainly developed in the United States in the early years of this century (i.e. after Rei-denberg and Lessig presented their concepts). Kal Raustiala assessed the via-bility of trans-governmental networks and evaluated their relationship to the liberal internationalism.[104] Based on studies of other market segments (than the Internet) the information exchanges among the competent authorities for sector-specific legal rules through the development of a set of direct interac-tions among sub-units of different governmental agencies can build appropri-ate network structures. Thereby, a disaggregation of States in favor of estab-

---

[98]   Weber, 2014a, 63 et seq.

[99]   For a more detailed analysis see Weber, 2014a, 64/65.

[100]   Hart, 1997, 94 et seq.

[101]   Foucault, 1978/79, ed. 2004, 29 et seq.

[102]   Teubner, 1989, 81 et seq.

[103]   Teubner, 1989, 118 et seq.

[104]   Raustiala, 2002, 17.

lished networks or a framework of "disaggregated sovereignty" can occur.[105] Correspondingly, even treaty compliance might gain better attention in a system of trans-governmentalism.[106]

The most prominent theoretical concept for interlinked networks has been developed by Anne-Marie Slaughter in her well-known book "A New World Order" offering a solution for the "governance dilemma" by referring to "governmental networks". These networks are set out as "relatively loose, cooperative arrangements across borders between and among like agencies that seek to respond to global issues".[107] Governmental networks manage to close gaps through coordination among governments from different States, thereby creating a new sort of power, authority, and legitimacy.[108] Since – according to Slaughter – governments cannot effectively deal with every issue in a networked world, the delegation of their responsibilities and "actual power to a limited number of supranational government officials"[109] who are able to engage in intensive interactions as well as in the elaboration and adoption of codes of best practice for coordinated solutions of common problems appears to be an adequate approach.

Such an approach corresponds to the mentioned theoretical concepts of legal philosophers (Hart, Foucault, Teubner) assessing networks as an answer to the existing differentiation and "autonomization" of systems.[110] Consequently, the structural conditions of the networks' (sub-systems') capacities gain importance.[111] However, for a transnational network to function properly, some conditions must be met, for example the proper definition of common rules and communication channels, a widely-shared regulatory philosophy, a high level of professionalism, and a sufficient amount of mutual trust.[112]

An additional dimension of formalized standards and networks concerns the complexity structures. Often the regulatory environment is embedded in a structural complexity matrix or several webs of normative guidelines.[113] Since

---

[105]   *Raustiala*, 2002, 10, 23/24 and 55/56.
[106]   *Raustiala*, 2002, 76.
[107]   *Slaughter*, 2004, 14.
[108]   *Slaughter*, 2004, 12/13; see also *Weber*, 2014a, 66.
[109]   *Slaughter*, 2004, 263.
[110]   *Teubner*, 2012, 159
[111]   *Luhmann*, 1975, 163.
[112]   See also *Senn*, 2011, 103, and *Benkler*, 2011, 721 et seq.
[113]   *Weber*, 2014a, 68.

regulatory models in these situations[114] may be converted into a hybrid nature, the best mix to obtain the desired outcome has to be selected. The respective regulatory modalities can be framed as follows:[115]

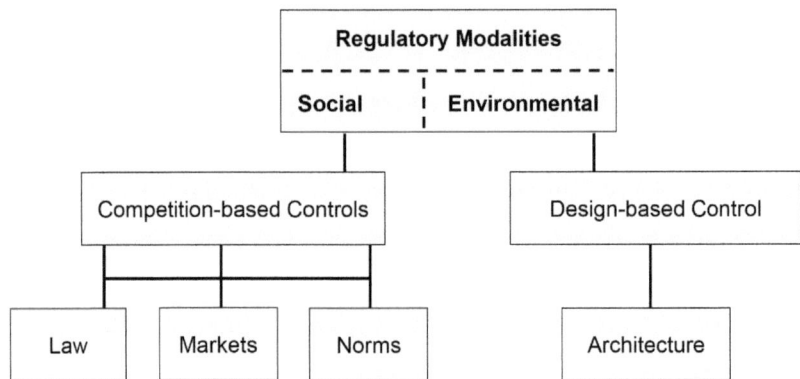

Depending on the regulatory needs, an even more-dimensional matrix can be developed that allows showing a regulatory intervention potentially occurring at any given point;[116] for such kind of regulatory matrix the term of "polycentric regulation" has been coined at a later stage.[117]

4.   Informal Law-making

The approach of law-making through informal social relations is based on the human's evolution from individuals into members of society that – already in the thinking of Socrates – consent to abide by the rules and principles of the State.[118] The subsequent emergence of personal property led to the development of social structures and the necessity of regulation.[119] Arguing that civil society needs governments to avoid living in the state of nature causing vio-

[114] See also *Lessig*, 1999a, 87/88.
[115] *Murray*, 2007, 37; see also *Weber*, 2014a, 68.
[116] See *Weber*, 2014a, 69, and *Murray*, 2007, 53/54, 236.
[117] See below Chapter III.C.1.
[118] *Plato*, ed. 1942, 77/78: see also *Murray*, 2007, 131/32.
[119] *Weber*, 2014a, 70.

lence and fear, already in 1651 Thomas Hobbes in his famous text "Leviathan" pleaded for the creation of "a new artificial person to whom all responsibility for social order and public welfare is entrusted".[120]

Thereafter, Jean-Jacques Rousseau, the main designer of the "social contract" theory,[121] demanded the conclusion of a social contract between all society members to help them to originate new forces.[122] Even though never pronounced aloud, the validity of the social contract, constituting everyone's personal will, must be implicitly accepted.[123] With regard to the fact that the cyberspace community is not a society being built based on a spontaneous gathering, the social contract approach cannot be applied directly but only by analogy.[124]

Since traditional formal law does not easily suit the need of Internet governance, informal norm-development gains importance. In the context of informality features of law-making, Joost Pauwelyn differentiates between three specific appearances of informal law-making:[125]

- *Process-informality*: This feature encompasses norms developed not in treaty-based international organizations but in often unstructured networks, fora and other groups.

- *Actor-informality*: This feature does not address the formal States representatives or diplomats but assesses the regulators, agencies or other entities including industry associations, private actors, civil society and similar informal networks.

- *Output-informality*: This feature looks at the norms being outside the traditional sources of international law such as standards, non-binding guidelines or indicators.

Informal law-making does not mean that international co-operation will no longer be of relevance, but a greater variety of law-making features, particu-

---

[120] *Hobbes*, 1651.

[121] *Rousseau*, 1754/1762; see also the description in *Weber*, 2009, 74 et seq.

[122] To this topic see *Weber/Weber*, 2009, 92.

[123] *Rousseau*, 1754/62, Book 1, Chapter 6, para 5.

[124] For further details see *Weber*, 2014a, 71-73.

[125] *Pauwelyn*, 2011, 126; see also *Weber*, 2014a, 74/75.

larly through less formal and less traditional channels, will be available.[126] As experience has shown, informal rules can set standards that are procedurally and substantially superior to formal law-making practices.[127]

Nevertheless, informal rule-making has to overcome some challenges: (i) The informality approach must maintain the laws' neutrality and protective force (in the interest of the weak persons) and comply with the rule of law concept in case of any limitation of freedoms. (ii) A balanced informality allowing effective co-operation with layers of accountability and control in a democratic society should be realized.[128]

A special approach in the informal rule-making context, developed by Warren Chik, has been described as "customary Internet-ional law". Thereby, the Internet-ional legal principles are based on the history of customs as a source of law.[129] Customary rules benefit from the recognition as legally legitimate (being established practices) and from the implementation as informal norms.

The foundation of customary rules can be seen in the Middle Ages' laws of the merchants ("*lex mercatoria*") and in the generally accepted "netiquette"; these rules are also recognized as a source of international law in Article 38(1)(b) of the Statute of the International Court of Justice.[130] Internet customs evolve out of necessity, practical functionality, and transactional efficacy; customs organically developed by the Internet community gain legitimacy as an autonomous normative framework.[131] The process of creating customs and then norms should not just be understood as the detection of behavior and attitudes of its participants but also as a special form of validating "norms" originating from the concerned persons.[132]

5. Normative Expectations

As stated by legal philosophers, law does not play a primary role in constituting societies; the main aspect is the self-constitution of a social system.[133] Never-

---

126 Pauwelyin, 2011, 127.
127 Pauwelyn, 2011, 129.
128 Pauwelyn, 2011, 137/38; see also Weber, 2014a, 75.
129 Chik, 2010, 10 et seq.
130 For further details see Weber, 2014a, 76/77.
131 Chik, 2010, 16.
132 See also Chik, 2010, 18/19.
133 Teubner, 2012, 103.

theless, normative expectations are usually based on generally accepted substantive principles helping to systemize or explain a set of legal rules and offering a reason for elucidating the object and the purpose of legal rules.[134]

In particular, according to Yochai Benkler the empowerment of individuals can lead to social production in form of a hybrid economy in the information environment that is marked by collaborative forms of development which are common-based or peer-produced (driven by decentralized creative inputs as evidenced by examples such Airbnb or Uber).[135] In the perception of Lawrence Lessig hybrid models are best suited to reflect current trends in global online interaction.[136]

The normativity context also looks at the involvement of civil society in the decision-making processes of the online world; obviously it is important to more closely analyze the democratic and participatory models. For example, the following approaches[137] have been developed: the "civic virtue" concept (David R. Johnson/David G. Post),[138] the "semiotic democracy" concept (Jonathan Zittrain),[139] and the "societal constitutionalism" concept (Gunther Teubner).[140] These concepts can build the foundations of transnationalism and cosmopolitanism theories.[141]

C. Second Generation Regulatory Models

Based on the first generation regulatory models new theoretical concepts have been developed in a second phase, reflecting the highly complex Internet ecosystem; the main approaches are shortly described hereinafter.

---

[134] Weber, 2014a, 82; see also Uerpmann-Wittzack, 2010, 1246/47.

[135] Benkler, 2006, 169; see also Weber, 2014a, 82/83.

[136] Lessig, 2008, 118, 248/49, 294; see also Kulesza, 2012, 148/49.

[137] For a more detailed discussion of these approaches see Weber, 2014a, 85-89.

[138] Johnson/Post, 1998.

[139] Zittrain, 2008, 147.

[140] Teubner, 2012, 46, 51/52.

[141] See below Chapter III.D.3 and 4.

1. Polycentric Regulation

As a consequence of the complexity situation[142] Internet regulations contribute to the evolvement of (complicated) structures.[143] In addition, regulatory competition can lead to webs of normative frameworks that support the further development of network structures.[144] Therefore, not surprisingly, Internet governance is moving from a static rule-making model to a dynamic regulatory matrix.[145]

This development and the chosen regulatory approaches have led to a "hypercomplex structural match".[146] Even if complexity is part of the concept of decentralization as it is based on networks of interdependencies, a decentered regulatory concept also causes fragmentation; a whole range of interactions among the State and civil society as well as among individuals and private organizations needs to be covered.[147] Such kinds of complex structures have been coined with the term "polycentric regulation" involving different communities in the rule-making processes.[148]

If the participants of polycentric regulation have a shared set of normative beliefs, notions of validity, and common policies, "epistemic communities" are growing.[149] In fact, the processes in the Internet ecosystem can be described as governance mechanism by transnational epistemic communities and networks, resulting in a polycentric structure; thereby, the Internet environment is in a position to improving connections and facilitating the exchange of communications.[150]

The polycentric regulatory concept's weakness consists in the practical problems of rule-making pluralism and fragmentation. The Internet is in need of an at least partially coordinated set of rules; discretionary pluralism would destroy the cyberspace's values since incompatible legal rules could have a

---

[142] See above Chapter III.B.4 (at the end).
[143] See also *Lessig*, 1999a, 91-93.
[144] *Murray*, 2007, 22 et seq.; see also *Weber*, 2014a, 89/90.
[145] *Murray*, 2007, 241.
[146] *Jørgensen*, 2013, 22-24.
[147] *Senn*, 2011, 31.
[148] *Murray*, 2007, 47 and 234/35.
[149] From a general regulatory perspective see *Braithwaite/Drahos*, 2000, 24 and 622/23.
[150] *Senn*, 2011, 170 with further explanations.

negative impact on its global reach.[151] In addition, the activities developed by epistemic communities and transnational networks raise issues of legitimacy and democratic deficit.[152]

Nevertheless, the approach chosen by the polycentric regulation model makes clear that rule-making activities concerning the Internet should not necessarily cover the whole range of possible legal issues. In addition to that, a functional differentiation following the needs and requirements at stake seems to be necessary. Instead of a territorial approach, a sectorial regime affiliation appears to be more appropriate in Internet rule-making; such kind of functional differentiation should be linked to the substantive regulatory topics in cyberspace.[153]

As a result, each of the functionally differentiated regulatory systems is based on its own operative rationality and should develop its own dynamics. The various ecosystems as well as the manifold designs and patterns of the concerned communities' interests can be reflected in the polycentric regulation. However, this social advantage goes hand in hand with a lack of coherence in the global Internet legal framework.[154]

2.   Hybrid and Mesh Regulation

A complex matrix of elaborate network structures can be seen as a combination of "hybrid" elements; "hybridity" reflects the attempt to elucidate the complexities of networks.[155] In regulatory theory, the term "hybrid" is described as a combination of a contradictory difference, marked not by either/or, but by both-and, guiding the search for new tendencies in law and society.[156] The approach of hybrid regulation can also help analyzing and understanding the limits of traditional legal categories and descriptions with the objective of trying to develop ways to reconcile any contradictions resulting from categorization.[157]

The concept of hybrid regulation is confronted with the weakness that it does not allow any assessment in respect of the question what interests are pur-

---

[151]   Weber, 2014a, 91.

[152]   Senn, 2011, 170.

[153]   Weber, 2014a, 92.

[154]   Senn, 2011, 254.

[155]   Weitzenboeck, 2014, 62; for a theoretical foundation see Weitzenboeck, 2012, 17 et seq.

[156]   Sand, 2009, 874.

[157]   Weitzenboeck, 2014, 65.

sued:[158] Individuals can act in their own interest or in a common interest shared by other stakeholders in order to reach an overarching network purpose. In view of the fact that the respective objectives are often not identical, procedural rules have to make transparent which interests are pursued by whom. In particular, a substantive system of checks and balances is needed in order to have a mechanism that allows balancing potentially differing interests.[159]

Another approach is the so-called mesh theory being based on the acknowledgement that a paradigm shift has occurred due to the profound transformation from a pyramid model with the government at the top to a network ("réseau") model.[160] This shift reflects the situation that the State sovereignty is not an intangible status anymore and that the will of the State legislator ceases to be received as a dogma; moreover, different powers need to interact (State, private enterprises, civil society).[161]

The move towards mesh regulation is considered to be founded on two major transformations in the legal and political landscape, namely (i) the weakened position of the statutes as the primary instrument of legal control and (ii) the increased use of the notion of governance instead of government.[162] The first transformation leads from a centralized sovereign authority to a flexible, decentralized, adaptive, and often negotiated regulation.[163] The second transformation causes a process allowing to coordinate the efforts of actors and social groups in fragmented and uncertain environments.[164]

Following this conceptual approach the theory of "network communitarism" can be described as a process of discourse and dialogue between the individual and society.[165] As a result, the concept of mesh regulation applied to complex technological networks that have overcome the divisional system of centralized sovereign State regulation leads to the insight that the relative importance of each source of rule depends on the nature of the activity and the other stakeholders (participants) being regulated.[166] Nevertheless, the regula-

---

158   Weber, 2014a, 92.
159   Weitzenboeck, 2014, 67.
160   Ost/van de Kerchove, 2002, 14.
161   Ost/van de Kerchove, 2002, 14.
162   For more details see Ost/van de Kerchove, 2002, 26-32.
163   Weitzenboeck, 2014, 69.
164   Ost/van de Kerchove, 2002, 29.
165   Murray, 2012, 68
166   Weitzenboeck, 2014, 72.

tory strength of this concept comes at risk in view of the fact that it leaves substantial discretion for the assessment of the quality of rule-making and does not give any guidance as to the values of the norms agreed by the communities.[167]

3.   Global Legal Pluralism Approach

A similar approach conceptualizing a world of hybrid legal spaces has been developed as the theory of "global legal pluralism".[168] This concept intends to encompass more than one legal, or quasi-legal, regime in the same social field. In a hybrid reality with overlapping legal spheres, the creation or preservation of multiple parallel legal systems might be an alternative; nevertheless, a precondition of this approach must be seen in the requirement that the involved actors acquiesce to procedural mechanisms, institutions or practices.[169] Legal pluralism envisages providing a *"jurisgenerative"* model that "focuses on the creative interventions made by various normative communities drawing on a variety of normative sources in ongoing political, theoretical, and legal iterations".[170]

The concept of "global legal pluralism" attempts at recognizing the normative conflicts between different regimes and at overcoming the differences by bringing the involved actors into a shared social space.[171] Nevertheless, a weakness of this legal pluralism concept consists in the uncertainty of being able to identify the applicable rules since clear guidance on how to substantiate the pluralism is missing.[172]

4.   New Experimentalist Model

Another quite recent theoretical approach trying to overcome the problems of previous regulatory concepts pleads for a "global experimentalist governance" (called "GXG process"),[173] an institutionalized transnational process of participatory and multilevel problem-solving that frames critical issues in an open-ended way by subjecting them to periodic revisions. Due to transna-

---

[167]   *Weber*, 2014a, 94.
[168]   *Berman*, 2007, 1158/59; see also *Weber*, 2020, 111.
[169]   *Berman*, 2007, 1162-1165.
[170]   *Berman*, 2007, 1166.
[171]   *Berman*, 2007, 1192/93.
[172]   See also *Weber*, 2014a, 94.
[173]   *De Burca/Keohane/Sabel*, 2014, 477-486.

tional corporations, other non-state entities, civil society and public-private partnerships entering into agreements, novel forms of regulation are rapidly developing alongside the previous forms of international law.

An ideal-type of GXG process comprises five key steps,[174] namely (i) the initial reflection and discussion among stakeholders; (ii) the articulation of a framework understanding with open-ended goals; (iii) the implementation of these broadly framed goals; (iv) the continuous feedback provided from local contexts; (v) the periodic and routine re-evaluation of the goals and practices including their possible adaptation and/or revision.

The GXG concept has certain similarities with the approaches of the polycentric, hybrid, and mesh regulation since it looks at complex multi-layer networks; however, GXG puts more emphasis on new forms of learning from implementation by showing how a practical understanding can be organized.[175] The justification of GXG lies in the fact that States have become unable to formulate a comprehensive set of rules and effectively monitor compliance; in addition, States must not be stymied by disagreement over basic principles and the co-operation of civil society actors either as agenda setters or as problem solvers is normally indispensable.[176] Furthermore, GXG appears to be likely not to work if the key actors are unwilling or reluctant to co-operate; nevertheless, a final appealing feature of GXG can be seen in its potential to increase participation in, and thus the democratic legitimacy of, institutions.[177]

A problem with the GXG approach consists in the vulnerability to manipulation and unintended consequences; in addition, the foreseeability and the predictability of legal norms appear to be low.[178] A further weakness can be seen in the fact that the link to the international legal setting is rather weak: even if cyberspace is considered a new world and if global experimentalist governance could be a challenging approach, manifold linkages to the (further) existing real or physical world continue to exist.[179] In other words, the conceptual discussions should more intensively address the relations between (theoretical) regulatory concepts and the decision on how to have them embedded into the ongoing (and developed) international normative order.

---

[174]   De Burca/Keohane/Sabel, 2014, 478.
[175]   De Burca/Keohane/Sabel, 2014, 478.
[176]   De Burca/Keohane/Sabel, 2014, 484.
[177]   De Burca/Keohane/Sabel, 2014, 484.
[178]   See also Weber, 2014a, 97.
[179]   See also Reed, 2012, 221.

D. Impacts of Theories on the Normative Framework

The description and discussion of the (first and second generation) regulatory models has shown that a wide variety of elements should be taken into account when designing the Internet governance ecosystem. In whatever form the Internet regulations will be established, the influence of technical codes, the (partly informal) network relations and standards, the polycentric matrix of involved actors, the mesh and experimentalist nature of rules, etc. merit attention in view of the objective to meet the needs of global pluralism. However, the available regulatory models addressing traditional rationales and social/technological changes do not give very clear guidance and do not solve existing political tensions. Nevertheless, the whole theoretical background must be kept in mind if rule-making by any legislative body is taken at hand.

In addition, irrespective of the chosen theoretical regulatory approach, the applicable rules must reflect the involvement of civil society in decision-making processes of the online world[180] rendering it imperative to more closely analyze the democratic perspectives within an appropriate legal order that mirrors the national and international needs of the involved actors. These aspects having a constitutional foundation are discussed hereinafter.

1. Conversion of Theoretical Concepts into Policies and Rule-making

Looking at the experience of the last few years, it seems obvious that the identification of the relevant political structures and their shortcomings as well as the assessment of the international legal order's potential is of importance.[181] Different perspectives should be analyzed, for example (i) the actor-oriented organizational aspects and (ii) the allocation of political power between the involved actors.

(i) An analytical framework of network governance can be based on two main "organizational" elements, namely the actors and the relations between the actors.[182] As far as the relations are concerned, several tensions exist, for

---

[180]   The participation processes will be discussed in detail below (Chapter IV.A.2).

[181]   See *Rioux*, 2013, 49-54, for an overview of the constellations of regulatory instruments in global governance; for a recent analysis looking at the knowledge governance see *Haggart*, 2019, 25 et seq.

[182]   See *Chin/Changfeng*, 2018, 8 et seq.

example formal vs. informal, strong vs. weak, direct vs. intermediary (broker, gatekeeper[183]), or mutual interests vs. conflicting interests. These tensions influence the power distribution (central ordering vs. structural equivalence).

Any kind of normative environment must address the mentioned tensions. Thereby, the appropriateness of the legal framework addressing Internet governance depends on the ability of the policy makers to embrace new approaches using different normative concepts and tools.[184] As a consequence, by linking democratic anchorage and regulatory authority in a feasible way, the implementation of the legal instruments must be done with great care and prudence in order to avoid undesired effects.[185]

(ii) Two visions of political power can be distinguished: the dominance of the State power as founded on the sovereignty concept and the power distribution relying on various stakeholders.[186] The two competing models have an impact not only on the international rule-making agenda but also on the design of supranational institutions and the role of sovereign States. Therefore, the decision for one of the two basic models influences the decision-making processes and, indirectly, the outcome of deliberations.

A good example is reflected in the different approaches pursued in connection with the interpretation of the term "Internet security" (robustness and stability on the one hand, public policy considerations on the other) at the World Conference on International Telecommunications in Dubai (WCIT, December 2012), organized by the International Telecommunication Union (ITU), as well as at the annual conferences of the Internet Corporation for Assigned Names and Numbers (ICANN).[187] Equally, the Plenipotentiary Conference of the ITU 2018 in Dubai did not adopt any proposal about the allocation of competences either to a (national) governmental or to a multistakeholder entity.[188]

---

[183] In respect of intermediaries, a more detailed typology must be developed leading from coordination to representation.

[184] As a complementary form to the multilaterism, *Brummer*, 2014, *passim*, developed the concept of a so-called "minilaterism" addressing smaller scopes of transnational understandings.

[185] See *Ewert/Kaufmann/Maggetti*, 2020, 184 et seq.; *Weber*, 2014a, 102; specifically to the network governance understanding from a Chinese perspective see *Chin/Changfeng*, 2018, 3 et seq.

[186] To the respective multistakeholder discussion see below Chapter IV.A.2.

[187] See *Weber*, 2013, 98, 101.

[188] See *Voelsen*, 2019, 25.

The current challenges in Internet governance regulation by nature require a broader and more collective decision-making than in a (national) State. In times of globalization, the movement towards global governance is unavoidable and the structure of international law will need some adaptations. However, as Rodnik has pointed out ten years ago, a fundamental political trilemma exist, namely between national self-determination, democracy, and "hyperglobalization"; usually not all three principles can be realized at once since the combination of any two elements excludes the third element.[189]

Therefore, the crucial point concerns the appropriate balance of power between sovereign States, non-state actors such as businesses and individuals, and new geographic or functional entities in a power-sharing framework.[190] A mechanism allowing to appropriately balancing the different interests becomes unavoidable. Such a mechanism must meet the legitimacy criteria as outlined hereinafter.[191]

(iii) As a result, in conciliating the different perspectives, global governance must enshrine collective efforts enabling the concerned persons to identify, understand, and address the global problems that go beyond the capacity of individual States to solve.[192] Insofar, the following aspects should be taken into account:[193] (i) A global framework needs to be combined with domestic political theory in order to assess the necessary interplay of the different levels. (ii) Political theories must be able to provide guidance as to what principles should be adopted and what principles should be implemented in reality. (iii) Rules are needed that help determine how general principles can be applied to specific issues.[194]

Consequently, such kind of normative concepts will be further elaborated by way of discussing three "modern" terms having been coined in connection with policies' deliberations, namely digital constitutionalism, transnationalism, and cosmopolitanism.

---

[189] Rodrik, 2010, 200.
[190] DeNardis, 2014, 23.
[191] Legitimacy is discussed in detail below in Chapter IV.A.1.3; see also Suzor, 2019, 238.
[192] Weber, 2020a, 109.
[193] Weber, 2014a, 105: see also Weber, 2013, 106.
[194] Caney, 2006, 2/3.

2. Digital Constitutionalism

Recently, the term "digital constitutionalism" has become a phenomenon of both transnational and national Internet rights advocacy.[195] With this term, the practice of envisioning, drafting and distributing documents that articulate "a set of political rights, governance norms, and limitations on the exercise of power on the Internet"[196] is described. The "constitutional moment" mainly concerns the availability of generally acknowledged principles governing the cyberspace environment. The actual source can be seen in the idea of global representation, the democratization of the transnational sphere and the possibility of improved outcomes of decisions.[197]

A "digital transnational constitution" does not exist in writing notwithstanding the fact that respective academic attempts have been undertaken. The main example is the concretization developed by Thelisson with the specific "Constitution for a Federation of the Internet".[198] This draft constitution has been prepared along the structure of a national constitution, encompassing

> – a purpose clause,
>
> – different rules about institutions and organizational competences of the Internet Federation,
>
> – provisions addressing democracy and the specific functions of the Internet Federation and
>
> – a detailed human rights charter.

This project of a "Constitution" for the Internet environment was not anymore pursued during the last few years but the respective ideas appear suitable to be deepened in academic research. In addition, "digital constitutionalism" certainly leads to the need of discussing transnationalism and cosmopolitanism.

---

[195] *Redeker/Gill/Gasser*, 2018, 302 et seq.; *Padovani/Santaniello*, 2018, 295 et seq.

[196] *Redeker/Gill/Gasser*, 2018, 303.

[197] *Hofmann*, 2016, 44.

[198] *Thelisson*, 2012, 89 et seq.

3.   Transnationalism

Civil society using the Internet does need a minimal legal order. Such kind of normative framework should have a cross-border nature since the Internet is a global infrastructure, i.e. it includes transnational legal rules. In substance, these rules might encompass non-binding standards, the so-called *"lex mercatoria"*,[199] common approaches or guidelines for institutional monitoring, and model laws.[200] Thereby, States should also recognize the efficacy of non-state norms. In principle, globalization of legal developments involving manifold legal sources leads to a shift of the focus of political engagement from "sovereign States" to "functional regimes".[201]

During the last few years, strategies of transnational advocacy networks in digital constitutionalism have been mobilized.[202] Global civil society in a transnational sphere encompasses activists, coalitions, non-governmental organizations (NGOs) and networks being able to counterbalance the cross-border activities of large (public or private) entities.[203] Relevant elements are shared values, dense exchanges of information, and a common discourse.[204]

Without any doubt, the rise of transnationalism is unavoidable in the Internet governance context.[205] In particular, norms put into the pipeline of "transnationalism" and achieving normativity in international relations[206] usually have certain common characteristics (such as legitimacy, clarity, and coherence).[207] These generally acknowledged characteristics governing the Internet ecosystem merit particular attention.[208]

4.   Cosmopolitanism

The concept of cosmopolitanism attempts at realizing the principle of a certain limitation or at least decentralization of State power in the interest of a more global appreciation. In this context Fukuyama states that "modern con-

---

[199]   See above Chapter III.B.4.
[200]   *Basedow*, 2008, 708.
[201]   *Shaffer*, 2012, 232.
[202]   See for example *Keck/Sikkink*, 1999, 89 et seq.
[203]   See also *Scholte*, 2004, 211 et seq.
[204]   *Keck/Sikkink*, 1999, 89.
[205]   *Weber*, 2016a, 206/07.
[206]   *Koskenniemi*, 2009b, 11.
[207]   See also *Fukuyama*, 2004, 98.
[208]   See *Weber*, 2015, 781/82.

stitutional government and the rule of law were established deliberately to limit discretion in the exercise of state power, as indicated by the phrase government by laws and not by men commonly attributed to Aristotle".[209] Assuming that this kind of global political system is the most effective way of implementing cosmopolitan principles of justice, an appropriate policy framework encompassing democratic and accountable global governance principles must be designed in an instrumental form.[210]

In view of the globalization of (inter-)governmental relations and of the governance frameworks, political theory refers to the notion of "cosmopolitanism" embracing three elements:[211]

–   *Individualism*: The ultimate units of concern are human beings and persons, rather than ethnic, cultural, or religious communities, countries, States, being units of concerns only indirectly, in virtue of their individual members or citizens.

–   *Universality*: The status of ultimate unit of concern is attached to every person being equal, not merely to some subsets of persons, such as men, whites, etc.

–   *Generality*: Persons are ultimate units of concern for everyone, not only for some individuals, such as compatriots and fellow religionists.

From this philosophical understanding the conclusion can be drawn that guiding principles for humanity do have a global nature, even if influenced by smaller entities.[212] The values that motivate both democratic and effective government at the domestic level also motivate some form of democratic and effective global governance.[213] Even without being a coherent set of norms, the existing public international laws having been evolved during the last few decades can lead into the direction of a global rule of law concept that is able to at least enshrine the basic principles of humanity's law.[214]

In the delineation of the substantive principles, a stronger focus should be directed to the concept of transnationalism. In overcoming the State-centricity of traditional law, "collective regulation operating among economic actors

---

[209]   *Fukuyama*, 2004, 98/99.
[210]   For a general overview see *Scholte*, 2004, 211 et seq. and *Benhabib*, 2006, *passim*.
[211]   *Pogge*, 1994, 89/90 with further references; see also *Weber*, 2013, 106.
[212]   *Weber*, 2013, 106.
[213]   *Caney*, 2006, 266.
[214]   *Weber*, 2015, 781; for further details see Chapter V.

or social groups with strong transnational ties and allegiances"[215] must gain importance. Not at least, transnational law supplies a larger storehouse of rules on which to draw[216] and allows designing governance patterns in not coherent structures. The presence of transnational law also indicates a flow of legal rules that is dynamic in form.[217]

The described fundamental issues (digital constitutionalism, transnationalism, cosmopolitanism) have not yet attracted the required attention in the inter-disciplinary discussions. More emphasis on these issues is needed; therefore, the referenced thoughts will be taken up in the context of the discussions of the appropriate international legal concepts that should govern Internet governance and the Internet ecosystem.

---

[215] Koh, 2006, 745; see also Cotterrell, 2009, 481/82.

[216] Philip J. Jessup, cited by Wolfgang Friedmann, Human Welfare and International Law – A Reordering of Priorities, in: Wolfgang Friedmann et al. (eds.), Transnational Law in Changing Society – Essays in Honor of Philip C. Jessup, New York/London 1972, 129/30.

[217] See also Senn, 2015, 494.

IV. Substantive Governance Principles

As mentioned, the society using the Internet does need a minimal legal order or normative framework, respectively. But the commented theoretical regulatory approaches do not offer fully suitable solutions that would suffice for establishing an adequate design which appropriately embraces a newly developed network infrastructure environment. Instead, more extensive guidance should be drawn from general substantive principles being conceptually able to complement the formal structures; therefore, light needs to be shed on some relevant substantive principles (such as legitimacy and participation, transparency, accountability). By purpose, apart from the more theoretical deliberations, the historical developments will be presented in detail.

A. Legitimacy and Participation

Legitimacy is the core of any governmental activities on the international and on the national level. If whatever kind of regulatory framework (be it hard law or soft law) is not based on a legitimate foundation, compliance with it by civil society cannot be expected. In order to improve the acceptability of implemented rules, participation of the concerned addressees in their development (in material substance and in equitable procedures) is crucial. In the Internet governance context new forms of participation gained importance.

1. Legitimacy: Traditional Foundation and Understanding

1.1. Notion and Contents

The word "legitimacy" can be traced back to the Latin word "*legitimus*" as meaning "lawful, according to law".[218] Legitimacy reflects an authority's right to rule and embraces the justification of ruling power giving the governed persons or entities the impression that their own values are represented in a decision-making context.[219]

---

[218] The sub-chapter A.1 on legitimacy is substantially based on *Weber*, 2020a, 111-113; a more detailed analysis of the legitimacy issues is contained in *Weber*, 2009, 105 et seq.
[219] *Weber*, 2014a, 102/03.

Legitimacy in a wider sense can also enshrine an ethical-philosophical dimension that installs legitimacy at a "higher" level than positive law. Usually a distinction is made between normative legitimacy theories, setting out general criteria for evaluating the right to rule, and empirical legitimacy theories, focusing on belief systems of those persons subject to regulation. As a result, legitimacy can be justified either by formal ideas as the rule of law rationale (legality) or by substantive value rationality based on morality and justice.[220]

The differentiation between source-oriented and procedure- or result-oriented types of legitimacy provides for further valuable approaches and foundations in the Internet governance context.[221] According to Jürgen Habermas, a source-oriented perception qualifies an authority as legitimate if it refers to the *demos*, the public.[222] Constructing such a legitimizing source from the manifold stakeholders involved in the governance of the Internet can build the appropriate framework for the multistakeholderism concept.[223]

Procedural steps (or adequate procedures, in the terminology of Niklas Luhmann[224]) within the different governing entities may enhance the legitimacy of policy-making decisions.[225] In this tradition Thomas M. Franck described legitimacy as "the aspect of governance that validates institutional decisions as emanating from a right process".[226] Therefore, legitimacy reflects the relevant elements of governance in a given setting.

1.2. Normative Character

Legitimacy must be designed in line with constitutional values and principles. As architectural pillars, three concepts can be put in place, namely "legality, morality, and constitutionality". These concepts appear to be suitable to "mark out the terrain within which the practice of legitimacy tends to take place".[227] Legitimacy plays the role of a reconciling norm, enabling consensus on how the three pillars are to be accommodated among each other.[228]

---

[220] See also *Clark*, 2005, 18/19.

[221] *Weber*, 2009, 110.

[222] *Habermas*, 1992, 117.

[223] See below Chapter IV.A.2.

[224] *Luhmann*, 1975, 9–53

[225] See *Weber*, 2009, 109/10, for a detailed analysis of the legitimacy of policy-making from a theoretical perspective.

[226] *Franck*, 1995, 1.

[227] *Clark*, 2005, 18.

[228] *Clark*, 2005, 19; see also *Braman*, 2020, 29 et seq.

The assessment of legitimacy can be done from different perspectives encompassing regulatory purposes, regulatory standards, regulatory instruments, regulatory effectiveness, and regulatory connection. These perspectives are gaining importance since legitimacy questions are becoming weightier not only for the international society in general but also for the stability of the international order.[229] In this sense, the rules designed to govern the Internet must have an overall legitimate purpose and should reasonably likely be efficient without going further than necessary to achieve that goal.[230] Thereby, legitimacy is not solely and specifically focusing on States but concerns all organizations having an impact on civil society. As a "virtual province", the Internet should mainly be "managed" through a bottom-up approach with a large number of stakeholders (principle of multistakeholderism).[231]

As mentioned, procedural elements are crucial for the acknowledgment of a right process. However, procedure must be complemented by a substantive conception that looks at the outcome of the legitimizing procedures (a result-oriented type of legitimacy). Such an approach depends on the values deemed as appropriate by the stakeholders concerned, thus justifying them as adequate procedures. To avoid subjective perceptions of legitimate values prevailing, Habermas tried to link the procedural aspects with specific notions of contents. This "discourse principle" assumes that those norms can claim validity that are approved by all potentially affected persons, insofar as they participate in a free and rational discourse.[232]

1.3. Concretization for Internet Governance

In Internet governance, the implementation of appropriate organizational rules in the concerned social communities is a necessity. The applied process can choose between different avenues. On the one hand, moral norms falling under the notion of netiquette are relevant for online macro-communities. On the other, the proper administration of the Internet, seen as a micro-community, needs some basic taxonomy.[233]

ICANN as the main organization in Internet governance is a private organization. However, over time its legitimacy increased, partly due to the loosening

---

[229] Weber, 2014a, 113/14.
[230] Suzor, 2019, 238.
[231] See Weber, 2014a, 114, and Clark, 2005, 12-17.
[232] Habermas, 1992, 161.
[233] Weber, 2014a, 112.

ties to the government of the United States, partly due to the increased participation by other stakeholders during the last years. Legitimacy encompasses
the international organizations and procedures as well as the participation of
the concerned (outside) actors. The improvement of the respective measures
related to the ICANN Board has been intensively debated and also reviewed by
expert groups. The most recent results can be found in the Third Accountability and Transparency Review Team (ATRT3) Report of May 2020.[234]

Apart from the realization of the ATRT3 recommendations,[235] further progress
in respect of the legitimacy requirements would obviously be possible, particularly regarding legal remedies (for example, an independent mediation and
arbitration system).[236] But the subsequent deliberations will concentrate on
the issues of participation, transparency, and accountability.

Looking from a theoretical and general perspective, it should also not be
underestimated that the traditional self-regulatory mechanisms addressing
organizational legitimacy issues have moved to aspects of a more democratic
and equally harder normative framework. Thus, the legal impact on governance elements has become stronger, and some quality criteria of regulation
are fulfilled to a wider extent. This development can be mainly seen in the context of the multistakeholder concept.

2.   Participation: Multistakeholderism as New Concept

A good governance needs to involve all concerned actors, particularly in the
context of a global infrastructure such as the Internet. Consequently, also
actors, traditionally not granted with sovereign power, for example business
entities, non-governmental organizations, and members of civil society need
to become part of decision-making processes. During the last years, the inclusion of all stakeholders in the legislative and governance processes has
become a hotly debated topic under the heading of "multistakeholderism".

---

[234]   Third Accountability and Transparency Review Team (ATRT3), Final Report, 108 et seq.
<https://www.icann.org/public-comments/atrt3-final-report-2020-06-16-en>; for fur-
ther details see below Chapter IV.A.2.4.

[235]   The internal legitimacy measures related to the ICANN Board will not be more deeply discussed hereinafter; in contrast, the focus will be laid on participation issues in the course
of the following sub-chapters.

[236]   See below Chapter IV.C.2.1.

2.1. Notion and Foundation of Multistakeholderism

Traditionally, legitimacy refers to States and organizations having governmental power. In the context of Internet governance, however, the relevance of additional stakeholders has been realized and (at least partly also) acknowledged. Manifold stakeholders are concerned and can play a role in the Internet ecosystem; therefore, the concept of multistakeholderism gained substantial importance.[237]

Before the second World Summit on the Information Society in November 2005 (Tunis), the Working Group on Internet Governance (2005) introduced a widely accepted working definition of multistakeholderism. This definition refers to the "development and application by governments, the private sector and civil society, in their respective roles, of shared principles, norms, rules, decision-making procedures, and programmes that shape the evolution and use of the Internet".[238] In line with this description, the interests of the stakeholders involved should be designed by participatory mechanisms reflecting the whole society's view.[239] Nevertheless, it should not be overlooked that multistakeholderism is not a completely new phenomenon evoked in the context of Internet governance; earlier developments concerned for example the labor and sustainability fields.[240]

In the context of mutlistakeholder concepts, different theoretical and practical issues can be raised, for example by way of the following four basic questions: How do the concerned groups reasonably match the challenges with the organizations, experts, and networks? How can governing bodies and entities be most able to help develop legitimate, effective, and efficient solutions? How should the flow of information and knowledge necessary for implement-

---

[237]   The sub-chapter (A.2) is based to a far extent on Weber, 2020a, 113-117; for an early analysis of the bottom-up concepts after the two WSIS Summits see Dany, 2008, 53 et seq. and Weber, 2009, 77 et seq.

[238]   Report of the Working Group on Internet Governance, June 2005, <www.wgig.org/docs/WGIGREPORT.pdf>.

[239]   Weber, 2012, 8; for a broad analysis of the multistakeholder model see Malcolm, 2008, passim.

[240]   For further details see Weber, 2016b, 247-249; to the concept recently also DeNardis, 2020a, 7/8 and Hofmann, 2020, 256 et seq.

ing appropriate governance be structured? How can different governance groups approach coordination between geographically different governance networks to avoid conflicting interests?[241]

Practical considerations lead to the following additional questions: How can greater transparency and dialogue between different civil society groups and standards' experts be introduced? How can standards be developed rapidly with the scrutiny of the increasing multistakeholder arrangements?[242] The mentioned questions are to be assessed in connection with the structuring of a multistakeholder decision-making framework as outlined hereinafter.

Basic values of multistakeholder models are openness (access to discussions, negotiations, and decisions), transparency (clear formal and substantive regimes with appropriate representation), accessibility (for information sources and procedures), accountability (responsibility of decision-makers), credibility (general acceptance of decision-makers), and consensus-orientation (acceptability of decisions taken).[243] These basic values should be the foundation for appropriate legitimacy strategies, but the schemes must be broad enough and leave room for adaptations in a given context.

2.2. Forms and Legal Framework of Decision-Making

The concept of multistakeholderism requires at least two classes of stakeholders.[244] Different concepts of multistakeholderism can be and are implemented in reality, subject to the types of actors that are involved and the nature of authority relations between these actors.

Depending on the design of the actors and the scope of relations, the combinations in a matrix can be manifold.[245] Furthermore, multistakeholder arrangements usually also vary by level. Four ideal-typical structural models have been developed: hierarchy (for example: International Telecommunication Union), homogeneous polyarchy (for example: Internet Engineering Task

---

[241]   ICANN/WEF Panel on Global Internet Cooperation and Governance Mechanisms, Panel Report: Towards a Collaborative, Decentralized Internet Governance Ecosystem, <https://www.icann.org/en/system/files/files/collaborative-decentralized-ig-ecosystem-21may14-en.pdf>.

[242]   *Brown/Marsden*, 2013, 200.

[243]   *Weber*, 2016b, 251.

[244]   *Raymond/DeNardis*, 2015, 572, 575; for a detailed analysis of the architectural principles and the processes of international regime formation see *Weber*, 2009, 89 et seq.

[245]   *Raymond/DeNardis*, 2015, 577, 583.

Force, W3C, International Organization of Securities Commissions), heterogeneous polyarchy (for example: ICANN, UN Global Compact), and anarchy.[246] Often, the choice of the models is limited, but some discretion for the involved stakeholders is mostly given. The development of completely new approaches is equally possible as Wolfgang Kleinwächter has shown with the conceptual comparison between the "United Nations" (governmental model) and the "United Constituencies" (civil society or multistakeholder model).[247]

In general, a multistakeholder decision-making framework should encompass the following main elements:[248]

- Identification of the most adequate set of stakeholders participating in a particular issue;

- Definition of the criteria and mechanisms for the selection of representatives from different groups;

- Avoidance of capture of multistakeholder processes by corporate power or influential nongovernmental organizations;

- Implementation of crowdsourcing techniques bringing inputs into dialogue on difficult topics;

- Establishment of technologies helping the representatives liaise with their constituencies and monitor reached agreements;

- Creation of a technological framework facilitating dialogue to reach a minimum consensus in a multistakeholder body;

- Methods for accelerating the decision-making processes in multistakeholder bodies;

- Theoretical models supporting consensus building and decision-making in multistakeholder environments.

---

[246] *Raymond/DeNardis*, 2015, 580, 603.

[247] See *Kleinwächter*, 2011, 571/72; this model has so far not attracted high attention but would merit to be deepened and worked out in a more detailed manner.

[248] See *Almeida/Getschko/Afonso*, 2015, 78.

In designing the multistakeholder decision-making framework, political contexts and cultural factors must be taken into account. The implementation should also consider the effect of existing standards on the decision-making of an organization and whether potential entry barriers for stakeholders can be lowered.[249]

A multistakeholder legal framework does not exist at this time; however, many international declarations and guidelines include aspects of multistakeholder regimes. The following examples are particularly noteworthy:[250]

–   *United Nations' "Protect, Respect and Remedy" framework* (so-called "Ruggie-Principles"): The Final Report of March 2011 addressing governments and private actors sets out basic guiding principles on business and human rights.[251]

–   *United Nations Guiding Principles on Business and Human Rights*: The UN Guiding Principles (2011) outline the implementation of the Ruggie Principles and how to better manage business and human rights challenges.[252]

–   OECD *Guidelines for Multinational Enterprises*: The 1976 introduced and 2011 revised OECD Guidelines invite private actors to implement standards for good practices in respect of responsible and sustainable supply chains.[253]

–   *ILO Framework*: The Tripartite Declaration of Principles Concerning Multinational Enterprises and Social Policy (edition 2017) does not only address States but also employers' and workers' organizations and contains guidelines regarding employment, conditions of work and life, and industrial relations, etc.[254]

---

[249]   See also *Weber*, 2016b, 250 and *van Huijstee*, 2012, 45.

[250]   For a more detailed overview see *Weber*, 2016b, 253-258.

[251]   Final Report, see
<http://www.ohchr.org/Documents/Issues/Business/A-HRC-17-31_AEV.pdf>.

[252]   See
<http://www.ohchr.org/Documents/Publications/GuidingPrinciplesBusinessHR_EN.pdf>.

[253]   OECD, Edition 2011, <http://www.oecd.org/daf/inv/mne/48004323.pdf>.

[254]   Declaration, <https://www.ilo.org/wcmsp5/groups/public---ed_emp/---emp_ent/---multi/documents/publications/wcms_094386.pdf.>.

Within the last 20 years, many Internet governance declarations, guidelines, and frameworks have been developed and published; most of them address participation by using the term multistakeholderism.[255] Generally looking the analysis shows that cultural and contextual factors play a role in shaping both the functioning and the outcome of multistakeholder processes.[256]

2.3. Concretization for Internet Governance

Practical experiences have shown over the last few years that a range of approaches, mechanisms, and tools are available for the realization of multi-stakeholder objectives, leading to the acknowledgment that a toolbox should be developed with a number of suitable instruments.[257] This assessment is not surprising since multistakeholder models must rely on an ever-increasing participation by those with interests, capacities, and needs.[258] Therefore, the multistakeholder concept may not be seen as a value in itself to be applied homogeneously to governance functions, i.e. it is not a one-size-fits-all solution.[259] However, the development of systems for sharing information, taking decisions, designing checks and balances, and implementing assurance models is at the heart of effective multistakeholder initiatives.[260]

Multistakeholderism is practiced in reality in, for example, the context of the Internet Governance Forum, which includes a special committee, the Multistakeholder Advisory Group (MAG), whose roughly 40 seats represents the five world regions and also balance gender.[261] The multistakeholder element, addressing participation in different ways and using different terms, also prominently appeared in the NETmundial Multi-stakeholder Statement released at the closure of the NETmundial Conference held in São Paulo in April 2014.[262] Attendees from around the world, i.e. governments, the private

---

[255] For an analysis of the manifold Internet governance declarations see *Rolf H. Weber*, Principles for governing the Internet: a comparative analysis, UNESCO Series on Internet Governance, Paris 2015.

[256] See *Weber*, 2016b, 258.

[257] *Gasser/Budish/West*, 2015, 2; see also *Buzatu*, 2015, 11-14.

[258] *Doria*, 2013, 135.

[259] *Weber*, 2016b, 258.

[260] *Buzatu*, 2015, 16.

[261] *Hofmann*, 2016, 16; see also *Raustiala*, 2017, 496.

[262] See <http://netmundial.br/netmundial-multistakeholder-statement/>.

sector, civil society, the technical community, and academia, drafted this non-binding statement. In the meantime, ICANN also partly opened the door for some multistakeholder exchanges, mainly in connection with accountability.[263]

Without any doubt, the debates about Internet governance and multistake-holderism must encompass the general and relevant policy issues, in particular legitimacy, transparency, and accountability; so far, the topics have only been linked in a limited way.[264] In addition, further aspects such as decision-making procedures,[265] formation and operation of the relevant organizations as well as effectiveness need further attention.[266] A particularly important factor is the degree to which a group is inclusive of a diverse array of stakeholders.[267] Inclusiveness means dynamic participation by being able to contribute to a discussion and to influence the final outcome (in the form of "voting").[268]

In view of these manifold factors, no standard way to form multistakeholder groups can be established. Depending on the cultural and the contextual factors in shaping the functioning and the outcome of governance groups (for example, the preexisting relationships between the stakeholders, the connection between the governance group and the governmental institution, the allocation of resources, and geopolitical factors), the actual dimensions of multistakeholder groups must be designed; therefore, a broad spectrum of purposes can be listed, ranging from open-ended missions to issue-specific tasks.[269]

Even if multistakeholderism is not a value as such, it must be considered as a possible approach for meeting salient public interest objectives as well as for realizing standards and values of a democratic understanding by determining what types of decision-making are optimal in the given functional and political context.[270] The following elements and action points support effective multistakeholder governance:[271]

---

263 For an overview see <https://www.icann.org/resources.accountability>.

264 *Weber*, 2016b, 259-262; see also *Gasser/Budish/West*, 2015, 10/11, 22/23, 26.

265 *Zingales/Radu*, 2017, 67.

266 *Weber*, 2016b, 262-264; see also *Gasser/Budish/West*, 2015, 11-13, 18-26.

267 *Gasser/Budish/West*, 2015, 18.

268 See *Weber*, 2016b, 263.

269 *Gasser/Budish/West*, 2015, 10, 25; *Weber*, 2016b, 258.

270 *Raymond/DeNardis*, 2015, 610; for a detailed analysis of the democracy elements see *Gleckman*, 2018, *passim*.

271 *Buzatu*, 2015, 28-31; *Weber*, 2016b, 265.

- Identification and articulation of purpose and objectives (appropriate setting of the stage);

- Identification of the players (adequate and precise definition of the stakeholders);

- Development of the applicable multistakeholder governance model;

- Definition of the envisaged procedural formation and operation principles and description of the scope of inclusiveness;

- Determination of the appropriate level of transparency;

- Implementation of accountability standards;

- Provision of guidance for the implementation of the agreed standards;

- Identification of a sustainable and credible funding model for the multi-stakeholder processes;

- Development of oversight and assurance mechanisms.

In a nutshell, multistakeholder initiatives can be seen as fora multipliers through manifold platforms for dialogue. Furthermore, such initiatives are suitable to establish fora for evolving standards and governing mechanisms.[272] But many factors in multistakeholder initiatives need further research; in particular, a multidisciplinary examination of the relevant questions incorporating socio-legal, economic, policy-oriented, and game theory studies, as well as interdisciplinary information studies drawing on political analyses appear to be indispensable.[273] Developing a multidisciplinary catalog of methodologies as well as the corresponding multidisciplinary instruments can improve the chances for the existence of an appropriate toolkit as well as the comprehension of challenges going along with a better participative decision-making and the configuration of governance concepts.[274]

---

[272]   Weber, 2020a, 117.
[273]   Brown/Marsden, 2013, 200/01.
[274]   Weber, 2016b, 265.

Subsequently, the realization and implementation of multistakeholder frameworks will be discussed in the context of ICANN and other Internet governance bodies; the respective (partly historical) deliberations may serve as specific case studies.

2.4. Participation Issues in ICANN

(1) Evolving Participation Regulations

Already more than ten years ago, the Affirmation of Commitments (AoC), addressed by the United States Department of Commerce to ICANN, referred in No. 4 to the existence of a multistakeholder development model acting for the benefit of global Internet users by highlighting the importance of ICANN to maintain and improve robust mechanisms and to make its decisions not just in the interest of a particular set of stakeholders but in the public interest.[275]

A specific approach adopted from national democratic frameworks could consist in the implementation of direct elections, usually seen as a mechanism to reduce the accountability deficit and the legitimacy problem. The original and early attempt of ICANN to integrate direct elections of (a part of) its Board into its organizational structure was deemed a failure and consequently stopped particularly due to the very small percentage of voting Internet users who actually participated in the elections.[276] However, whether the decision to terminate that experiment was in fact the right one, remains doubtful, especially because the other option of encouraging the public to vote was not even given a chance. The untried option would admittedly have contributed to an improvement of participation.

Leaving aside the mentioned voting option, other alternatives have been pursued during the last ten years in order to take up the AoC promise:[277]

---

[275] Affirmation of Commitments, September 30, 2009, <https://www.icann.org/resources/pages/affirmation-of-commitments-2009-09-30-en>.

[276] De Vey Mestagh/Rijgersberg, 2006, 29.

[277] As far as the descriptions in the sub-chapters to participation, transparency, and accountability are mainly of a historical nature, a smaller printing is used by purpose.

In March 2014 the U.S. Commerce Department's National Telecommunications and Information Administration (NTIA) declared "its intent to transition key Internet domain name functions to the global multistakeholder community" so as to "support and enhance the multistakeholder model of Internet policymaking and governance"[278] and asked all interested global stakeholders to develop a proposal for a transition scheme of the current role played by NTIA in the coordination of the Internet's domain name system (DNS). In so doing, the NTIA emphasized that the transition proposal must have broad community support and must (i) support and enhance the multistakeholder model, (ii) maintain the security, stability, and resilience of the Internet DNS, (iii) meet the needs and expectation of the global customers and partners of the IANA services and finally (iv) maintain the openness of the Internet.

After starting the IANA transition process at its public meeting in Singapore in March 2014, ICANN established the IANA Stewardship Transition Coordination Group (ICG) in July 2014, having been composed of 30 individuals representing 13 communities. For accomplishing their mission of coordinating the development of a proposal among the communities, the ICG outlined a charter for its future work.[279] Since the IANA functions were divided into three main categories, namely domain names, number resources and other protocol parameters, the ICG (among others) suggested to working on the different categories in parallel. The ICG wanted to serve as a "central clearinghouse for public information" during the whole transition process being charged with the task to confirm that the proposals meet the NTIA requirements and are supported by broad community consensus.

Having targeted the end of the IANA contract in September 2015, the ICG alerted the involved communities of their responsibility to develop plans for a prompt IANA transition. After being provided with a Request for Proposals (RfP) by the ICG on 8 September 2014[280] setting forth the NTIA requirements each of the three communities developed and delivered a response to the ICG.[281] Hereinafter, the ICG combined these three documents and issued a call for public comments on the combined transition proposal on 31 July 2015. Having received 157 comments from a wide variety of stakeholders, most of whom (65%) were either supportive of the proposal or expressed qualified support accompanied with questions or criticism, the ICG published a Summary Report on Public Comments Received on 30 November 2015.[282] The respective comments

---

[278] NTIA Announces Intent to Transition Key Internet Domain Name Functions, Press Release, 14 March 2014, <http://www.ntia.doc.gov/press-release/2014/ntia-announces-intent-transition-key-internet-domain-name-functions>.

[279] Draft charter for the IANA Stewardship Transition Coordination Group, 17 July 2014, <https://www.icann.org/en/system/files/files/draft-charter-coordination-group-17jun14-en.pdf>.

[280] See <https://www.icann.org/en/system/files/files/rfp-iana-stewardship-08sep14-en.pdf>.

[281] ICG, Proposal to Transition the Stewardship of the Internet Assigned Numbers Authority (LANA) Functions from the U.S. Commerce Department's National Telecommunications and Information Administration (NTIA) to the Global Multistakeholder Community (ICG Proposal), October 2015, pp. 32-210.

[282] ICG, Summary Report on Comments Received during the Public Comment Period on the Combined Transition Proposal (ICG Summary Report), 30 November 2015, online available at: <https://www.ianacg.org/icg-files/documents/Public-Comment-Summary-final.pdf>.

mainly touched issues like jurisdiction, root zone maintenance, compatibility and interoperability, accountability and workability but also participation; on that regard "an overwhelming majority of commenters stated their belief that the proposal supported the multistakeholder model".[283]

The following Annual Reports emphasized ICANN's increased public participation concept in a multistakeholder model by referencing to the organization's continuously bigger number of attendees and the provided services enabling Internet users to add their voices to the discussions from wherever they are (remote participation).

(2) Assessment of Further Activities

Apart from the possibility to reconsider the mentioned approach of having an electronic vote on the composition of the Board, other measures could also be taken into account. ICANN seems to be aware of the need to come closer to civil society. A geographic move into this direction was the opening of branches in Singapore and Istanbul, governing the East Asian and the Eastern Europe/Western Asian regions. Furthermore, upon the call of the Brazilian government to have a special Summit on different issues in Internet governance, ICANN immediately responded in a positive way and called for a multistakeholder initiative in the preparation of this Summit which was held in São Paulo in April 2014 (NETmundial).[284]

Undoubtedly, the design of multistakeholder participation depends on the given factual situation. Even though multistakeholderism is no longer a new phenomenon, a debatable and critical aspect of this approach still consists in the concretization of multistakeholders' inclusion and participation.[285] Based on the experiences of the last years, multistakeholder advocates need to identify and describe the objectives of this approach afresh: for a better understanding it is important "to analyze (i) what the organizations do (ii) how they do it (iii) what characteristics, values, and best practices are widely shared among these organizations".[286] In this context, an assessment of the "success" would be worth-wile to conduct, encompassing the stated and executed functions of multistakeholder organizations, the scope and scale of existing problems, the diversity of participation, and the incentives to participate, as well as the role of, or relation to, sovereign entities.[287]

---

[283] ICG Summary Report (supra note 282), 7.

[284] See also above Chapter IV.A.2.3.

[285] See Doria, 2013, 115 et seq.

[286] Waz/Weiser, 2013, 341.

[287] Weber, 2013, 103.

The new modes of multistakeholder governance must also gain democratic accountability by constituting a link between the public sphere and civil society. Such link should include the media-based critical public debate of operations and outcomes, which may function as a (diffuse) corrective.[288]

Subsequently, ICANN also aimed at increasing its collaboration with other Internet groups such as the Internet Society, the Internet Engineering Task Force and the Internet Governance Forum. The provision of good remote participation services, enabling Internet users to participate at the discussions of its meetings from wherever they are, equally leads to increased and improved participation. In the context of the ICANN's strategic objective to deal with the multistakeholder model evolution, 26 recommendations were adopted by the ICANN Address Supporting Organization's (ASO) independent reviewers together with other bodies having the objective to provide for a strengthened ASO participation during all ICANN meetings.[289]

Already the Affirmation of Commitments (2009) limited the influence of the United States Department of Commerce (US DoC) on ICANN and the Internet regulations substantially. The IANA stewardship transition of 2016 has then been the final step in a nearly two decades long process (starting in 1998) conducted by the US DoC in order to transition the coordination and management of the domain name and addressing systems to the private sector, i.e. to ICANN.[290] Since 2016, not anymore a country or several countries is/are "controlling" the Internet but the community of Internet stakeholders is coordinating the respective systems.

The most recent attempt of supporting a broad participation approach can be seen in the launch of the "Enhancing the Effectiveness of ICANN's Multistakeholder Model" initiative in April 2019.[291] Notwithstanding the fact that the ATRT3 diagnosed a certain stagnation in the public participation of civil society regarding the involvement in developing ICANN management issues, its Report contains a substantial number of recommendations, suggestions and observations being suitable to strengthen and increase the public input in the

---

[288] *Héritier/Lehmkuhl*, 2011, 138.

[289] For the ASO participation records see <https://aso.icann.org/aso-ac/meetings/aso-ac-meeting-participation-records/>.

[290] IANA Stewardship Transition, September 30, 2016, <https://www.internetsociety.org/iana-transition/>; see also *Raustiala*, 2017, 491 and 499.

[291] See <https://www.icann.org/resources/pages/governance-plan-improve-multistakeholder-model-2019-04-08-en>.

future.[292] ICANN confirmed to take up the submitted proposals; the envisaged bottom-up approach with all concerned stakeholders has in the meantime also influenced the ICANN Strategic Plan for Fiscal Years 2021-2025 published in October 2020.

2.5. Participation in Other Internet Governance Bodies

(1) International Telecommunication Union

For the first time in the history of the Telecommunication Union, some civil society representatives were invited to attend the 2012 World Conference on International Telecommunications (WCIT) in Dubai.[293] This invitation can be considered as an important step towards multistakeholderism. However, the negotiations in Dubai have also shown that some countries such as Russia, China or Saudi Arabia are attempting to subordinate the management of the Internet to governmental control, mainly by referring to issues such as security and public order.[294] Bearing in mind that national control is not only a political, but also a technical issue, such kind of development would lead to a (national) fragmentation of the Internet.[295]

In this context the so-called "Iranian Internet Resolution" needs to be taken into account having been submitted to the plenary session at the WCIT by some Arab Countries.[296] After almost two weeks of fruitful discussions, the Iranian representative called for a vote on the inclusion of a "right of access of Member States to international telecommunications services" into the International Telecommunication Regulations (ITR) Preamble.[297] Having been adopted by a majority decision and included in the ITR Preamble, Western media have presented this amendment as an attempt to deviate from a global infrastructure governed by a multistakeholder approach.[298]

Being of the opinion that the multistakeholder approach represents the best opportunity to regulate the Internet, the United States and some allied countries envisaged to only implement

---

[292]   ATRT3 (supra note 234), 41 et seq. and 134 et seq.

[293]   *Weber*, 2013, 98.

[294]   *Weber*, 2013, 99.

[295]   See below Chapter V.A.3.

[296]   Arab States Common Proposals, Document 64(Add.23)-E, November 2012, <http://www.internetgovernance.org/wp-content/uploads/T09-WTSA-12-C-0064.pdf>.

[297]   *Weber*, 2013, 99; see also *Raustiala*, 2017, 500.

[298]   *Weber*, 2013, 99.

modifications of the existing ITR regulations. In this context, the US aimed at including general principles with the objective of widening the ITR's scope towards the whole Internet framework which was opposed by the sovereignty-oriented countries.[299]

Even though the potential implementation of multistakeholderism has been partly perverted during the WCIT's negotiations since (i) many important motions were discussed in closed rooms and (ii) civil society representatives were hardly heard in the plenary sessions, the WCIT's opening can be seen as being an important step into the direction of a broader participation of all interested stakeholders. Furthermore, the list of attendees' enhancement helps to increase the WCIT's transparency and accountability.

Since the WCIT 2012, the ITU is more inclined to invite a broader spectrum of stakeholders to the annual conferences held at its domicile in Geneva.[300] This positive development appears to be more likely realizable in daily and technical matters than in politically sensitive affairs as the results of the Plenipotentiary Conference of ITU in 2018 (Dubai) have shown.[301]

(2) *Internet Engineering Task Force*

Referring to itself as being a "large open international community of network designers, operators, vendors, and researchers concerned with the evolution of the Internet architecture and the smooth operation of the Internet", the IETF is "open to any interested individual".[302] Accordingly, the entity lives the multistakeholder approach to a far-reaching extent.

---

[299] Apart from some "extreme" positions, a good number of ITU Member States such as India, Brazil, South Africa or Egypt fell in between the two camps; following neither of the above mentioned positions regarding the governance of the Internet, they reject Internet censorship and closed networks. They are also critical of the role of the United States and of the big Internet companies on the Internet; see in this context *Andreas Klimburg*, The Internet Yalta, Commentary, Centre for a New American Security, 5 February 2013, p. 2, <http://www.cnas.org/publications/commentary/the-internet-yalta>, and *Wolfgang Kleinwächter*, Internet Governance Outlook 2013: "Cold Internet War" or "Peaceful Internet Coexistence"?, CircleID, 3 January 2013, <http://www.circleid.com/posts/20130103_internet_governance_outlook_2013/>.

[300] For a general (older) assessment of the participation and involvement of civil society in ITU matters see *Irion*, 2009, 87 et seq.; see also *Raustiala*, 2017, 496/97.

[301] See *Voelsen*, 2009, 25.

[302] See IETF, About the IETF, <http://www.ietf.org/about/>.

(3) WSIS *Forum*

With governments realizing the growing importance of the new information and communication services, the ITU passed a resolution in 1998 proposing the idea of a World Summit on the Information Society (WSIS) under the auspices of the United Nations.[303] One of this Summit's main goals was to bridge the global digital divide separating rich/developed countries from poor/less developed countries. In 2001 the ITU Council endorsed the approach of holding the Summit in two phases, the First Summit in Geneva (2003), the Second Summit in Tunis (2005).

The WSIS started as an intergovernmental process. With regard to the fact that public participation helps to increase the transparency (and accountability) of the governing bodies, the invitation of all relevant UN-related organizations and other international organizations, non-governmental organizations, civil society and private sector entities to actively participate at the WSIS was seen as valuable step towards a better involvement of all concerned actors. During the Second Summit in Tunis the multistakeholder concept as developed by the Working Group on Internet Governance (WGIG) referring to the roles and responsibilities of the various stakeholders such as governments, the business world, civil society and the academic/technical community was adopted.[304] Thereby, the interests of the parties involved should not be defined by any specific group, but through (procedural) participatory mechanisms reflecting the views of the whole society.[305]

For implementing the two Summits' findings, since 2006 an annual WSIS Forum is held in Geneva,[306] co-organized by ITU as main organization since the beginning together with UNESCO, UNDP and UNCTAD. The WSIS Forum is a global multistakeholder platform facilitating the implementation of the WSIS Action Lines. This body usually is preparing the contents of the Internet Governance Forum (IGF) and is hosting so-called High-Level Events (for example in 2014)[307]. In general, due to the IGF-oriented tasks, the years being deci-

---

[303] Resolution 73 of the ITU Plenipotentiary Conference.

[304] Working Group on Internet Governance (WGIG), Report of the Working Group on Internet Governance, June 2005, <http://www.wgig.org/docs/WGIGREPORT.pdf>.

[305] *Weber*, 2012, 8.

[306] Exceptionally also in New York (2015); due to the pandemic situation the WSIS 15 (2020) was held online.

[307] For more details see <http://www.itu.int/wsis/implementation/2014/forum/>.

sive for the prolongation of the IGF were particularly important for the WSIS Forum. Therefore, the WSIS 10 in 2015 and the WSIS 15 in 2020 had a specifically dense agenda.[308]

The documents agreed upon and issued by the WSIS Forum are not guidelines or recommendations in a legal sense being directly applicable in the Internet governance context but they are designed by way of inducing other bodies to implement the expressed ideas. Issues of participation are obviously dominant due to the multistakeholder involvement. An example related to the WSIS activities is the United Nations General Assembly's Outcome Document of 16 December 2015 recognizing the importance of multistakeholder co-operation, referring to the still existing need to promote greater participation and engagement of all stakeholders in the ongoing discussions on Internet governance and emphasizing the lack of woman's full participation in the decision-making processes.[309]

(4) *Internet Governance Forum*

During the Second Summit in Tunis, the WSIS did not only lay the foundation for the WSIS Forum but also called for the creation of the Internet Governance Forum (IGF); the mandate for the IGF is contained in the Tunis Agenda.[310] The IGF may "identify emerging issues, bring them to the attention of the relevant bodies and the general public, and, where appropriate, make recommendations", but does not have any direct decision-making authority.[311] In April 2006 the UN General Assembly published its endorsement of a five-year mandate of the IGF.[312] The first IGF took place in Athens from 30 October to 2 November 2006.

Towards the end of the first mandate, the UN initiated an evaluation assessing the merits of the IGF continuation; thereafter, the UN General Assembly adopted a second resolution prolonging the IGF for another five years.[313] A similar step was taken, based on an Outcome Document containing a 10-year-

---

[308]   See <https://www.itu.int/net4/wsis/forum/2020/>.

[309]   See United Nations General Assembly, Outcome Document, A/RES/70/125, Nos. 6, 27, 29, 54, 57, 61.

[310]   Tunis Agenda for the Information Society, <http://www.itu.int/wsis/docs2/tunis/off/6rev1.html>.

[311]   Mandate of the IGF, para. 72 of the Tunis Agenda, <http://www.intgovforum.org/mandate.htm>; for further details see *Weber*, 2009, 66 et seq.

[312]   UN General Assembly Resolution 60/252 of 27 April 2006.

[313]   UN General Assembly Resolution 65/141 of February 2011.

review of the implementation of the WSIS results, in late 2015; the UN General Assembly High-Level Meeting (WSIS 10) agreed to continue the IGF for a third period of now ten years,[314] with the commitment to address substantive issues during a special IGF Retreat in July 2016. The organizational structure of the IGF is composed of a (large) Multistakeholder Advisory Group (MAG) and a Secretariat located in Geneva, Switzerland. From 2006 to 2019 the fourteen IGF were physically held (Athens, Rio de Janeiro, Hyderabad, Sharm El Sheikh, Vilnius, Nairobi, Baku, Bali, Istanbul, João Pessoa, Guadalajara, Geneva, Paris, Berlin); the 2020 IGF became an online event due to the pandemic situation.

The yearly IGF is composed of the main or focus sessions and complemented by workshops or meetings of the practically important "Dynamic Coalitions", Best Practice Forums, and Open Forums. Preparatory efforts are usually done at the regional IGF (for example EuroDig) or at national IGF. The agenda of each IGF is driven by the interests and requests of the participants (in the meantime more than 2000 physically attending persons) and often channeled through the MAG. Obviously, the topics change subject to the given Internet governance "environment". In Athens themes like openness, security, diversity, and access were dominant. In the meantime other topics such as enhanced co-operation, multistakeholderism, emerging issues, inclusiveness and diversity, as well as sustainability in a broadly understood way gained importance.[315]

In the context of the participation topic it can be easily noted that the IGF is a very good example for the implementation of the multistakeholder approach allowing all interested actors, from governments, businesses, academia to civil society, etc. to contribute to the outcome of the debates and analyses.[316] However, as mentioned, the IGF is not a decision-making authority; therefore, from a strictly democratic perspective, the IGF does not realize a full participation model.

---

[314] See <https://publicadministration.un.org/wsis10/GA-High-Level-Meeting>.

[315] The results of the IGF 2020 are summarized in "IGF 2020: Final Report", <https://dig.watch/events/igf2020/final-report>. In general, the substantive issues cannot be analyzed and discussed in this book; for an overview see the IGF website, <https://www.intgovforum.org>. An excellent analysis assessing the IGF transcripts of 12 years by big data analytics and text mining has been recently published by *Cogburn*, 2020, 185 et seq.

[316] See also *Weber*, 2009, 66 et seq.; for the further development of the IGF see below Chapter VI.

B. Transparency

With regard to the fact that die Internet offers valuable opportunities for communications and that open access to discussion topics should be achieved, transparency merits more extensive consideration.

1. Notion and Types of Transparency

Transparency is central, both as a goal of regulation and as an attribute of the regulatory system.[317] The importance of transparency stems from its relevance for the achievement of other important tenets of regulation, such as independence and accountability of regulators. "Transparency facilitates compliance, effectiveness and the ability to access both".[318] In light of these findings, transparency has become a key issue within private enterprises and governmental organizations, both on national and international levels, and has been acknowledged to be a crucial issue when addressing the effectiveness of international regimes.[319]

Being defined as "easily seen through or understood"[320] transparency is usually assessed as encompassing characteristics such as clarity, accuracy, accessibility, and truthfulness. In so doing, transparency is an important topic in many market segments by among others enabling access to the information necessary for the evaluation of opportunities and costs of operation in a specific market.[321]

Often transparency is differentiated into three main pillars, namely procedural transparency, decision-making transparency and substantive transparency.[322]

- *Procedural transparency* encompasses rules and procedures in the operation of organizations that must be clearly stated, have an unambiguous character, and are publicly disclosed. In addition, they should make the

---

[317] For a general overview see *Weber*, 2008, 342 et seq.

[318] *Mitchell*, 1998, 111.

[319] *Weber*, 2008, 344/45.

[320] See Oxford Dictionary under the keyword "transparency".

[321] U.S. Proposal for Transparency Disciplines in Domestic Regulation: Building on Existing International Disciplines and Proposals (JOB(04)/128), dated 15 September 2004, para 1.

[322] *Weber*, 2008, 344.

process of governance and rule-making accessible and comprehensible for the public. An important aspect of the procedural transparency is the due process principle.[323]

- Being based on the acknowledgement of access to political mechanisms, *decision-making transparency* can be seen as reasoned explanations for decisions that, together with public scrutiny, are able to strengthen the institutional credibility and legitimacy of governmental decisions.

- *Substantive transparency* is directed at the establishment of rules containing the desired substance of revelations, standards and provisions which avoid arbitrary or discriminatory decisions. In addition to that, substantive rules often include requirements of rationality and fairness.

Besides the aforementioned distinction, various "directions" of transparency are discussed.[324] With regard to the principal's and the hierarchical subordinate's position, a distinction can be made between transparency upwards, transparency downwards, transparency outwards and transparency inwards.

- *Transparency upwards* is given if the hierarchical superior/principal is in a position to observe the conduct, behavior, and/or "results" of the hierarchical subordinate/agent, usually in a principal-agent relation.

- Conversely, *transparency downwards* puts the "ruled" into a position to observe the conduct, behavior, and/or "results" of their "rulers"; this relationship is often reflected in democratic theory and practice under the umbrella of the later presented "accountability".

- *Transparency outwards* describes a situation in which the hierarchical subordinate or agent is in a position to observe what is happening "outside" the organization.

- *Transparency inwards* addresses the freedom of information meaning that those outside are in a position to observe what is going on inside the organization.

The different pillars of transparency as well as the various "directions" of transparency can be found in the Internet governance context.

---

[323] Weber, 2008, 344.
[324] See Heald, 2006, 27/28.

2. Enhancing Transparency for the Future of Internet Governance

For building confidence in ICANN as well as in other Internet governance bodies enhancing transparency is a viable objective. Therefore, the historical development of the transparency efforts will be outlined; the observations are presented as form of examples how international bodies can proceed and what challenges need to be overcome. The main example is ICANN having already gone through three detailed review processes.

2.1. Transparency Issues in ICANN

ICANN's Bylaws[325] presently acknowledge the following transparency provisions: Art. III Sec. 1 (Purpose of Transparency) states that the corporation "shall operate to the maximum extent feasible in an open and transparent manner and consistent with procedures designed to ensure fairness". In addition to this, No 7 of the so-called "Core Values" of ICANN reads as follows: "Employing open and transparent policy development mechanisms that (i) promote well-informed decisions based on expert advice, and (ii) ensure that those entities most affected can assist in the policy development process" should guide each of ICANN's decisions and actions.

Beyond that, no. 9.1 of the Affirmation of Commitments (AoC)[326] between the US Department of Commerce and ICANN seeks to ensure transparency by stating that "ICANN commits to maintain and improve robust mechanisms for public input, accountability, and transparency so as to ensure that the outcomes of its decision-making will reflect the public interest". For facilitating transparency and openness in its deliberations and operations, ICANN is also obliged to publish "the terms and outputs of each of the reviews for public comment" (No. 10).

---

[325] ICANN, Bylaws for Internet Corporation for Assigned Names and Numbers (ICANN Bylaws), <http://www.icann.org/en/about/governance/bylaws>.

[326] Affirmation of Commitments by the United States Department of Commerce and the Internet Corporation for Assigned Names and Numbers, <http://www.icann.org/resources/pages/governance/aoc-en>.

(1) Findings of the First Accountability and Transparency Review Team

The Accountability and Transparency Review Team (ATRT) established in 2010 for implementing the Affirmation of Commitments' conditions divided its mission of reviewing ICANN's accountability and transparency between four Working Groups whose assignments were determined by subject matter.

The Working Groups (WG) were assigned to review (i) the ICANN Board of Directors' governance, performance, and composition; (ii) the role and effectiveness of the Governmental Advisory Committee (GAC) and its interaction with the ICANN Board; (iii) the public comment processes and the policy development processes; and (iv) the review mechanisms for Board decisions.[327]

Transparency and accountability have certain features in common; in particular, transparency through the making available of reliable information being accessible both logistically and intellectually is a condition for accountability. Therefore, the ATRT was assessing transparency and accountability in parallel.

With regard to transparency, the 2010 published report of the first Accountability and Transparency Review Team (ATRT1)[328] contains 27 (final) recommendations on how ICANN could improve its accountability and transparency; they are phrased as suggestions for the improvement of several existing transparency regulations.

By referring to the Nominating Committee's (NomCom) deliberations and the decision-making processes, recommendation no. 3 of ATRT1 suggests to clearly articulate "the timeline and skillset criteria at the earliest stage possible before the process starts and, once the process is complete, explain the choices made". Whereas recommendation no. 23 of ATRT1 among others seeks for a restructuring of the three existing review mechanisms for board decisions' recommendations, namely the Independent Review Panel (IRP), the Reconsideration Process and the Office of the Ombudsman, recommendation no. 26 of ATRT1 addresses the adoption of "a standard timeline and format for Reconsideration Requests and Board reconsideration outcomes that clearly identifies the status of deliberations and then, once decisions are made, articulates the rationale used to form those decisions". Additionally, the "overarching recommendation" no. 27 of ATRT1 concerns the Board's obligation to analyze ICANN's accountability and transparency performance and to publish an annual report to the community on progress made.[329]

---

[327]   Accountability and Transparency Review Team (ATRT1), Final Recommendations, December 2010, <http://www.icann.org/resources/pages/atrt-final-2010-12-31-en>.

[328]   ATRT1 (supra note 327).

[329]   Thereafter, apart from summarizing the efforts of ATRT1, the Annual Report 2012 of ICANN stated that all 27 recommendations were accepted by the ICANN Board and were implemented (p. 16).

(2) Assessment of the Second Accountability and Transparency Review Team

Complying with the mandate of the Affirmation of Commitments (AoC), a second Accountability and Transparency Review Team (ATRT2) was compiled in 2013. This review team's field of duties included three essential tasks, namely the evaluation of the already existing recommendations' implementation,[330] the development and submission of new recommendations to the ICANN Board and the contribution of suggestions on how to improve the review process.[331]

By highlighting the importance for ICANN to successfully implement the ATRT1's recommendations, the ATRT2 suggests ICANN to "establish itself as the benchmark of accountability and transparency". For ensuring the organization's viability in the long run, the ATRT2's Report addresses ICANN (i) to establish clear assessment criteria to measure improvements in its accountability and transparency mechanisms, (ii) to communicate clearly and regularly about all these processes, and (iii) to improve the current review processes.[332]

According to the Report of the ATRT2 the corresponding efforts were undertaken by the ICANN Board and it has become standard operating procedure for the Board to conduct consultations as well as information sharing sessions with respect to the Board's skill-set requirements.[333] Additionally, the Report refers to the fact that by adopting transparency guidelines as standard transparency procedure, the ICANN Board took a step forward to improve the organization's transparency. By among others highlighting the strengthening of the dialogue across the community the ATRT2 rates the implementation of recommendations 3 and 26 of ATRT1 as largely successful.[334]

In respect of the not fully implemented recommendation 23 of ATRT1, the ATRT2 argued that the review mechanisms should be a "final guarantee" encompassing an extensive support for the decisions made but "should not be seen as a way to solve process logjams at this stage alone".[335]

With regard to the Governmental Advisory Committee's recommendation of spending more attention to the accountability and transparency of ICANN's finances, the ATRT2 reached the finding that the organization "should develop new transparent and accountable mechanisms that combine more effective resource allocation and use with the involvement of all parties within the

---

[330] Three prior reports were at stake, namely the report of the first Accountability and Transparency Review Team (ATRT1, supra note 327), the report of the WHO IS Policy Review Team and the report of the Security, Stability and Resiliency (SSR) Review Team.

[331] Accountability and Transparency Review Team 2 (ATRT2), Final Report and Recommendations for Public Comment, 9 January 2014, <https://www.icann.org/public-comments/atrt2-recommendations-2014-01-09-en>.

[332] ATRT2 (supra note 331), 2.

[333] ATRT2 (supra note 331), 12/13.

[334] ATRT2 (supra note 331), 14 and 48.

[335] ATRT2 (supra note 331), 48.

multistakeholder model".[336] For accomplishing this goal, the ATRT2's report suggests ICANN to better control its financial governance structure by basing the organization's yearly budget on a multi-annual framework containing information regarding all activities planned and the respective expenses. With regard to the Ombudsman's operations, the ATRT2 is of the opinion that "ICANN needs to reconsider the Ombudsman's charter and the Office's role as a symbol of good governance to be further incorporated in transparency processes".[337]

Concerning possible improvements of the existing review process itself, a certain "review fatigue" due to the review's frequency is diagnosed by ATRT2. In order to avoid an undermining of its organizational effectiveness ICANN should consider alternative review approaches. Aspects requiring further consideration are for example the determined period of time to accomplish the review process and the procedure of how data flows find their ways from ICANN to the review team.[338] With regard to the organization's transparency enhancement, the ATRT2 among others recommends ICANN to publish its budget prior to each upcoming review.[339]

Subsequently, the ICANN repeatedly emphasized the importance of being a transparent and accountable entity; respective findings are contained in the Annual Reports of 2013 and 2014. ICANN launched new features on its MyICANN website and opened additional hub offices and engagement centers (after Singapore and Istanbul also in Beijing and in Montevideo). Furthermore, ICANN started to provide some annual statistical reporting on two key areas, namely the Documentary Information Disclosure Policy (DIDP) and the organization's internal anonymous Hotline for Reporting on Work-related Concerns.[340]

(3)   Findings of the Third Accountability and Transparency Review Team:

The Third Accountability and Transparency Review Team Report, for several unforeseen reasons including the pandemic of 2020 slightly delayed, but published in May 2020, is a very detailed document (almost 350 pages). However, notwithstanding the fact that accountability and transparency are dealt with in parallel for most parts it becomes obvious that transparency has comparatively lost a part of its significance, being also due to the positive developments in this field over the last few years. All over all, the ATRT3 has come to the conclusion that the accountability and transparency framework has substantially evolved since the ATRT2 Review was completed in 2013.[341] Even if not

---

[336]   ATRT2 (supra note 331), 62 and 65.
[337]   ATRT2 (supra note 331), 48.
[338]   ATRT2 (supra note 331), 57.
[339]   ATRT2 (supra note 331), 60/61.
[340]   See <https:/www.icann.org/resources/pages/governance/transparency-en>.
[341]   ATRT3 (supra note 234), 7.

all of the 46 ATRT2 recommendations were implemented, the effectiveness of the taken measures is qualified as being acceptable, in particular as far as the accountability and transparency suggestions relating to strategic and operational plans are concerned.[342]

In respect of transparency, the ATRT3 mainly proposes to change the Public Comment proceedings. The relevant documents should clearly identify, who the intended audience would be, provide a clear list of precise questions in plain language and develop further types of transparent participation possibilities; however, the priority of this recommendation is considered to be relatively low.[343] Furthermore, connected to accountability issues an improvement of transparency is also recommended in respect of ICANN's strategic and operational plans.[344]

2.2. Transparency in Other Internet Governance Bodies

Transparency issues equally concern other bodies playing a role in the Internet governance context; even if accountability issues have become more important over the last few years, the following transparency aspects merit to be mentioned:

(1) International Telecommunication Union

The multilateral organization being in its regulatory activities quite close to Internet governance is the International Telecommunication Union (ITU), a specialized agency of the United Nations.[345] Encompassing a public-private partnership concept the ITU, to date, has a membership of 193 countries and over 700 private-sector entities and academic institutions.[346] The ITU's Charter is referring to the "growing importance of telecommunication for the preservation of peace and the economic and social development of all States".[347] i.e. the ITU mainly has technical tasks.

---

[342] ATRT3 (supra note 234), 8.

[343] ATRT3 (supra note 234), 9/10.

[344] ATRT3 (supra note 234), 27/28.

[345] Historically, the "ITU model" and the "Internet model" have been polar opposites; the ITU mainly was an organization of States, the IGF a multistakeholder forum. For the participation issue see above Chapter IV.A.2.5.

[346] See <http://www.itu.int/en/about/Pages/default.aspx>.

[347] Constitution of the International Telecommunication Union (ITU Constitution), Preamble, <http://www.itu.int/net/about/basic-texts/index.aspx>.

Due to the fact that the organization is composed of States and private sector entities with no civil society participation, the entity's transparency has traditionally been relatively restrictive. Aiming at renewing the then existing International Telecommunication Regulations (ITR) as developed in 1988, the Member States of the ITU assembled at the World Conference on International Telecommunications (WCIT) in Dubai in December 2012. Prior to this event, for the first time in the ITU's history, the organization made a good part of the negotiation documents available (and therewith transparent) to the public and also invited some civil society representatives to attend the conference.[348] During the negotiations, the main problems occurred between the States, civil society representatives did not play a remarkable role.[349]

(2) Internet Engineering Task Force

In the Internet environment, technical standards have an important function. Therefore, even if policy-making is not the main driver of engineers, the importance of the Internet Engineering Task Force (IETF) and the Internet Architecture Board (IAB), among others watching over the IETF's activities, may not be underestimated. The way, how standards are designed and implemented, plays a crucial role, as the attempt of the IETF to introduce new encryption measure in the aftermath of the NSA surveillance disclosure has shown.

Mainly consisting of engineers with knowledge of networking protocols and software the IETF aims at establishing high quality and relevant technical documents that show how people design, use, and manage the Internet. Following the statement at the IETF plenary session of 1992 that the IETF "reject(s) kings, presidents and voting" and in comparison "belief(s) in rough consensus and running code", the IETF's first cardinal principle (open process) highlights the importance of any interested individual being able to participate in the IETF's work.[350] Having no members but participants the IETF discusses everything in topic specific areas,[351] everyone interested should "know what is being decided, and make his or her voice heard on the issue".[352] According to its own

---

[348] See *Weber*, 2013, 98.

[349] See *Weber*, 2013, 99/100.

[350] Internet Engineering Task Force (IETF), Mission Statement, <http://www.ietf.org/about/mission/>.

[351] See *Doria*, 2013, 132/133.

[352] IETF, Mission Statement (supra note 350).

commitment the IETF makes all documents, mailing lists, attendance lists and meeting minutes publicly available on the Internet; therewith, the IETF is not just talking about transparency but is also acting in a transparent way.

(3) WSIS Forum

As mentioned,[353] the WSIS Forum is pursuing the realization of the objectives adopted by the two WSIS in 2003/2005. Even if transparency does not appear to play a key role, the corresponding topics regularly are on the agenda of the WSIS Forum. As an example, the Outcome Document 2015, inspired by the WSIS Forum and adopted on 16 December 2015 as "Outcome Document of the High-level Meeting of the General Assembly on the overall review of the implementation of the outcomes of the World Summit on the Information Society" repeatedly refers to transparency.[354]

Stating that the creation of among others transparent and predictable legal systems would lead significant progress in connectivity and sustainable development in many countries, the Outcome Document also emphasizes the need to promote greater participation and engagement in the discussions on Internet governance and calls for strengthened, stable, voluntary and more transparent funding mechanisms.[355]

(4) Internet Governance Forum

As mentioned,[356] the Internet Governance Forum as multistakeholder platform without any decision-making power is a reasonably transparent body. So far, debates about transparency were not prevailing since it can be assumed that this substantive principle did not cause any major problems (similarly to the WSIS Forum).

---

[353] See above Chapter IV.A.2.5.

[354] United Nations General Assembly (A/RES/70/125) of 1 February 2016.

[355] A/RES/70/125 (supra note 354), Nos. 29 and 61.

[356] See above Chapter IV.A.2.5.

C. Accountability

Apart from to the aforementioned transparency aspects, functioning accountability mechanisms merit further attention in the context of international institutions and of Internet governance.

1. Notion and Elements of Accountability

Generally speaking, accountability[357] encompasses the obligation of one person to give account of, explain and justify his/her actions or decisions to another person in an appropriate way. Accountability is a pervasive concept, including political, legal, philosophical, and other aspects, each of them casting a different shade on the meaning of the term.[358] Together with checks and balances, accountability constitutes a prerequisite for legitimacy and a key element of any governance discussion.[359] While checks and balances take place by providing mechanisms to prevent the abuse of power, accountability steps do so by providing for or accessing actions with mechanisms such as non-judicial remedies, or judicial review.[360]

As a fundamental principle, accountability concerns itself with power and power implies responsibility. In so doing, accountability can be framed along three elements: (i) the provision of information in a timely manner, (ii) the introduction of standards that hold governing bodies accountable, and (iii) the implementation of mechanisms of sanction. Serving as a basic guideline as to what key elements must be included in a legal framework, accountability measures for governing bodies can have a concretizing function in respect of adequate corporative structures.[361] Additionally, accountability needs to include the democracy element of global governance if the outcome of the decision-making processes should be acceptable to civil society in general.[362]

Accountability can be assessed from an internal and an external perspective. Internally, the concerned stakeholders must have possibilities of participating in the procedures and filing a complaint in case of non-compliance; externally the question becomes relevant to what extent outsiders are entitled to be

---

[357] To the linguistic and historical insights see *Möldner*, 2019, 30 et seq.
[358] For a general overview see *Weber*, 2011, 133 et seq.
[359] *Möldner*, 2019, 37 et seq.
[360] For further details see *Kaufmann/Weber*, 2010, 791-796.
[361] See also *Weber*, 2014a, 78 with further references.
[362] See also *Scholte*, 2004, 211 et seq.

involved into the general framework of an organization.[363] At the international level, the need for accountability proportionally rises with the degree of autonomy and power exercised as can be shown as follows:[364]

	Internal accountability		
	Ex ante control (e.g. mandate, appointment)	Ongoing control (e.g. participation, veto)	Ex post control (e.g. budget, regulation, sanction)
No network autonomy or power (de jure or de facto)	No / less need	Complete	No / less need
Full network autonomy or power (de jure or de facto)	Crucial	Non-existing	Crucial

From a general perspective, effectiveness and accountability do not need to be (or to be perceived as) polar opposites: Effective co-operation requires accountability measures; and the core goal of accountability is an increased effectiveness learning from the feedback of the concerned stakeholders.[365]

2. Enhancing Accountability for the Future of Internet Governance

2.1. Accountability Issues in ICANN

In its own early documentation, ICANN distinguishes three types of accountability which encompass three ways of actions,[366] namely (i) public sphere accountability dealing with mechanisms for assuring stakeholders that ICANN behaves responsibly, (ii) corporate and legal accountability covering ICANN's obligations under the applicable normative systems and its Bylaws as well as (iii) participating community accountability that seeks to ensure that the Board and the executive bodies perform functions in line with the wishes and expectations of the ICANN community.

---

[363] Pauwelyn, 2011, 132/33.

[364] Pauwelyn, 2011, 136; see also Weber, 2014a, 80.

[365] Weber, 2014a, 80.

[366] ICANN, Accountability & Transparency Frameworks and Principles, January 2008, 4, <https://www.icann.org/en/about/transparency/acct-trans-frameworks-principles-10jan08-en.pdf>.

By stating that ICANN should be accountable for all its actions to the whole Internet community and obliging the organization to "operate in manner that is consistent with these Bylaws" (Art. IV Sec. 1),[367] accountability is determined as being one of ICANN's foundation pillars. In view of the implementation of this commitment, Art. IV Sec. 2 ICANN Bylaws states that any person affected by an action of ICANN needs to be entitled to submit a request for reconsideration or review of that action. With regard to Board actions a separate process for independent third-party reviews is established (Art. IV Sec. 3 ICANN Bylaws). In addition, ICANN's structure and operations are exposed to a periodic review (Art. IV Sec. 4 ICANN Bylaws).

ICANN provides three avenues for review of Board and staff decisions, namely two institutions, the Ombudsman and the Independent Review Panel (IRP), and the Reconsideration Process; to varying degrees, each mechanism is aimed at increasing ICANN's accountability. According to Art. V Sec. 2 ICANN Bylaws, the Ombudsman "shall serve as an advocate for fairness" in cases in which the Reconsideration Request and the IRP "are intended to reinforce the various accountability mechanisms otherwise set forth in Art. IV Sec. 3 ICANN Bylaws".[368]

(1) Findings of the First Accountability and Transparency Review Team

Each of the ATRT1's Working Groups[369] studied issues connected with accountability, but Working Group 4 addressed the most controversial issues of all.[370]

Its assignment to analyze mechanisms for appealing corporate decisions confronted the Board with the stark fact that none of ICANN's existing accountability review mechanisms allowed an appeal against a Board decision to an independent body with binding authority.[371] In this context, the WG4 among others referred to the assessment that the Request for Reconsideration is not handled independently of the Board and that decisions in response to such a Request do not bind the Board.[372] However, the WG4's attempt to challenge ICANN was (very exceptionally) rejected by the full ATRT1.

---

[367]   ICANN Bylaws (supra note 325).

[368]   To the weaknesses of the framework see *Weber/Gunnarson*, 2012, 14 and 21.

[369]   See above Chapter IV.B.2.1.

[370]   *Weber/Gunnarson*, 2012, 20.

[371]   *Weber/Gunnarson*, 2012, 14.

[372]   AoC/ATRT Working Group 4, Findings and Recommendations (Draft of 8 October 2010), <https://community.icann.org/display/atrt/Findings and Recommendations>.

Claiming that ICANN is not sufficiently supported by accountability mechanisms the ATRT1's (final) report concludes that "despite the importance accorded to considerations of accountability for ICANN, there is neither a standard working definition of accountability nor agreements on metrics to monitor and measure progress".[373] In addition to this, the ATRT1 claims that despite of ICANN's Bylaws, the internal strategy papers and the Annual Reports referring to accountability, a consistent accountability framework would still be missing.[374]

Several of the ATRT1's 27 recommendations deal with ICANN's accountability. Apart from an improvement of the decision-making process in the Board, the necessity of a comprehensive assessment of the accountability of the three existing mechanisms (Independent Review Panel, Reconsideration Process and Ombudsman) and their interrelation is expressed. In addition, according to the ATRT1 the operations of the Ombudsman and his relationship to the Board of Directors should be assessed and with regard to the reconsideration mechanism the standard for Reconsideration Requests should be clarified.[375]

(2) Assessment of the Second Accountability and Transparency Review Team

With regard to the Board's governance improvements, the ATRT2 stated that ICANN undertook several appropriate actions (in co-operation with the ICANN Nominating Committee).[376] In respect of the dispute resolution mechanisms, the assessment was generally more reluctant; partly the recommendations of ATRT1 were only incompletely implemented.[377]

In its Annual Reports, ICANN repeatedly emphasized the importance of accountability mechanisms and referred to the work of the ATRT2. Reference is also made to the fact that enhancing transparency makes tracking easier and therewith increases ICANN's accountability.

The ATRT2 has correctly identified the weaknesses in the ICANN's accountability framework. However, the recommendations could go even further and call for the implementation of more intensive requirements. In democratic States, accountability is typically bolstered through institutional checks and balances. The implementation of consultation processes could help streamline the realization of envisaged policies; the inclusion of civil society allows potential disputes to be addressed at an early stage and to look for solutions within due time.[378]

---

[373] ATRT1 (supra note 327), 81.

[374] ATRT1 (supra note 327), 81.

[375] The ICANN Board was quite reluctant to accept the findings of ATRT1 by arguing that the accountability mechanisms would be better than anticipated, however, a certain "pressure" to comply with the recommendations remained in place.

[376] ATRT2 (supra note 331), 9.

[377] ATRT2 (supra note 331), 10 and 48.

[378] See Weber, 2002, 114.

Civil society should not only be consulted in the preparatory phase of any project, but also be informed after its implementation. Feedback mechanisms concerning reviewing processes need to be consistently utilized being an aspect which would allow the participants in the process to understand how their insights and expertise have influenced the policy outcomes. The open communication of governing bodies improves the stakeholders' confidence, and transparent minimum quality standards enhance the assessment of performance and accountability; making activities and achieved results accountable to the "public" is particularly important with regard to the participation of civil society. The Internet governance bodies can only be held to account if their activities are visible and subject to evaluation. Therefore, accountability should also extend to monitoring stages related to actually executed efforts and empower the development of effectiveness through citizens' participation.[379]

Furthermore, accountability must enable the enforcement of principles by way of disciplinary measures and sanctions, thus attaching costs to the failure of meeting the expected standards.[380] Such kind of "sanctioning" should be based on the possibility of the concerned persons to get hold of the relevant information constituting the basis for redress.[381]

(i) Civil law accountability mechanisms encompass legal remedies to claim compensation for losses. Providing effective grievance mechanisms for those who believe that they have been harmed contributes to restoring trust in the business system. A minimum framework would have to include legitimacy with regard to the decision-making courts, fair, equitable and accessible procedures, and predictability of judicial outcomes. (ii) Widely accepted criminal standards could help implement legitimizing structures and the guideline for governance principles; experience shows that compliance with standards is generally increased by the threat of criminal sanctions in the case of violations.

In addition, the ICANN Board should not act as the ultimate arbiter of its own disputes.[382] Reconsideration can be worth-wile if it provides the Board with a genuine second look at decisions that were made in haste or without all the facts. The improvement of the Ombudsman system might support the search for amicable settlements. Nevertheless, a court-like body is indispensable. If no personal relationship exists and outstanding legal qualifications of the judges are guaranteed, the rendering of adequate review decisions can be expected.[383]

After the submission of the ATRT2 Report, ongoing efforts attempting at improving the accountability situation were taking place. Recognizing the importance of improving its own accountability, ICANN published a proposed process on "Enhancing ICANN Accountability", among others suggesting the

---

[379] For further details see *Weber*, 2002, 114.

[380] *Weber*, 2002, 117.

[381] See also *Weber*, 2011, 137.

[382] *Weber/Gunnarson*, 2012, 69.

[383] *Weber/Gunnarson*, 2012, 71.

formation of an ICANN Accountability Working Group (WG).[384] Based on the received (mainly positive) 49 comments[385] and the oral community dialogues at the ICANN-50 meeting in London,[386] a new document was published ("Enhancing ICANN Accountability – Process and Next Steps"), describing the process to examine, how the organization's accountability mechanisms should and could be strengthened.[387] Based on these efforts, two community groups were formed, namely an "ICANN Accountability and Governance Cross Community Group" and an "ICANN Accountability and Governance Coordination Group".

Even if the processes have slowed down subsequently, the Cross Community Working Group on Enhancing ICANN Accountability (CCWG-Accountability) published three draft proposals for recommendations in 2015;[388] the CCWG-Accountability identified a number of elements that needed to be in place and would form the accountability mechanisms, such as a revised Mission Statement for the ICANN Bylaws clarifying what ICANN does, an enhanced Independent Review Process for ensuring that ICANN stays within its Mission, an empowered ICANN community, a community Independent Review Process and some additional new powers.[389] The CCWG-Accountability also established a number of requirements necessary to enhance ICANN's accountability including among others the revision of ICANN's Bylaws, a reflection of the Affirmation of Commitments, the establishment of a set of fundamental Bylaws, the recognition of ICANN's respect for human rights, ICANN's commitment to implement the core set of accountability improvements and its willingness to discuss additional accountability improvements in 2016.[390] The CCWG-Accountability also emphasized in its Final Report that no intention exists to changing ICANN's bottom-up multistakeholder model.[391]

The comparatively smaller ICANN Accountability and Governance Coordination Group (CWG) was responsible for the categorization of issues including those identified by the CCWG-

---

[384] See ICANN, Enhancing ICANN Accountability: Opportunity for public dialogue and community feedback, 6 May 2014, <https://www.icann.org/en/system/files/files/enhancing-accountability-06may14-en.pdf>.

[385] See ICANN, Enhancing ICANN Accountability and Governance – Process and Next Steps, 14 August 2014,
<https://www.icann.org/resources/pages/process-next-steps-2014-08-14-en>.

[386] See <http://archive.icann.org/meetings/London2014/en/schedule/thu-enhancing-accountability.html>.

[387] See ICANN, Enhancing ICANN Accountability and Governance – Process and Next Steps (supra note 385).

[388] CCWG-Accountability Draft Proposal on Work Stream 1 Recommendations (Third Draft Report), 30 November 2015,
<https://community.icann.org/en/system/files/files/draft-ccwg-accountability-proposal-work-stream-1-recs-30nov15-en.pdf>.

[389] Third Draft Report (supra note 388), 5.

[390] Third Draft Report (supra note 388), 6.

[391] Subsequently, the CCWG-Accountability was mandated to work on a second report which was delivered in 2018.

Accountability and for building solution requirements for issues with input from the CCWGAccountability.[392] Having been formed as an integral part of the whole transition process the CWG's task was to develop a proposal for the elements of the IANA stewardship transition[393] that directly affect the naming community.[394]

(3) Findings of the Third Accountability and Transparency Review Team

As already mentioned, the Third Accountability and Transparency Review Team Report of May 2020 focuses more on accountability than transparency.[395] In an overall assessment the ATRT3 Report comes to the conclusion that most recommendations and suggestions submitted by the ATRT2 have been implemented even if some minor improvements would still be outstanding.[396]

In particular, the ATRT3 has reviewed the (herein not to be further discussed) ICANN accountability indicators in detail.[397] The results of this inquiry will have to accompany the ICANN Board in the future. Furthermore, specific attention has been paid to the assessment of periodic (now specific) and organizational reviews to be conducted in shorter intervals.[398] Another part of the recommendations concerns the accountability measures relating to strategic and operational plans;[399] these recommendations are signaled with high or at least medium priority.

An important accountability aspect concerns the enforcement of binding obligations and also a potential "sanctioning". Legal doctrine has argued during many years that insofar relevant weaknesses would exist within ICANN.[400] The

---

[392] See ICANN, Enhancing ICANN Accountability and Governance – Process and Next Steps (supra note 385).

[393] See above Chapter IV.A.2.4.

[394] For further details see <https://community.icann.org/display/gnsocwgdtstwrdshp/CWG+to+Develop+an+IANA+Stewardship+Transition+Proposal+on+Naming+Related+Functions>.

[395] See above Chapter IV.B.2.1.

[396] For further details see ATRT3 (supra note 234), 108 et seq.

[397] The indicators are described in a specific analysis contained in Annex C of the Report: ATRT3 (supra note 234), 218 et seq.

[398] For further details see ATRT3 (supra note 234), 8, 11, 18/19, and 83 et seq.

[399] ATRT3 (supra note 234), 11/12 and 27/28.

[400] See Weber/Gunnarson, 2012, 69 et seq.

ATRT3 has also looked into this aspect and assessed the Independent Review Process (IRP);[401] however, specific recommendations are not submitted which does not seem to be very convincing.

Since the main part of the ATRT3 Report relates to accountability issues and formulates many recommendations, their realization will be subject to discussions and debates during the next months and years. Because ICANN seems to be serious about the implementation in this field, optimism appears to be justified that the accountability will be further improved.

2.2. Accountability in Other Internet Governance Bodies

(1) International Telecommunication Union

In order to "protect and support everyone's fundamental right to communicate"[402] the International Telecommunication Union (ITU) is made up of three sectors, encompassing specific areas of ICT activities, namely Radiocommunication (ITU-R), Telecommunication Standardization (ITU-T)[403] and Telecommunication Development (ITU-D). With regard to the organization's object of "promoting broadband roll-out, forging tomorrow's technical standards, managing global spectrum and negotiating international frameworks for cybersecurity", it is hardly surprising that the demand for accountability mechanisms features quite often in the ITU's basic texts[404].

By way of example, Resolution no. 145 concerning the participation of observers in conferences, assemblies and meetings of the ITU States refers "the importance of ensuring the accountability of the Council to the Member States of the Union". In addition, the ITU's Independent Management Advisory Committee (IMAC) "must add value and must assist in strengthening accountability and governance functions of the Council and the Secretary-General"; for achieving this, members of the IMAC "should collectively possess knowledge, skills and senior-level experience in (among others) accountability structure" (Annex to Resolution no. 162). In practice, however, the level of accountability cannot be considered as being very high.

---

[401]   ATRT3 (supra note 234), 51 et seq.

[402]   See ITU, About ITU, <http://www.itu.int/en/about/Pages/overview.aspx>.

[403]   See <https://www.itu.int/en/ITU-T/Pages/default.aspx>.

[404]   See ITU, Collection of the basic texts of the International Telecommunication Union adopted by the Plenipotentiary Conference, 2011, Message from the Secretary-General, online available at: <http://www.itu.int/pub/S-CONF-PLEN-2011>.

(2)   Internet Engineering Task Force

The Internet Engineering Task Force (IETF) describes itself as "a loosely self-organized group of people who contribute to the engineering and evolution"[405] of the Internet. Thereby, the efforts attempt "to avoid policy and business questions, as much as possible".[406] Even though explicit accountability mechanisms are missing – the IETF "exists as a collection of happenings, but is not a corporation and has no board of directors, no members ..." – some rules and guidelines exist which make the organization work, as for example laid down in the Internet Standards Process RFC 2026.[407] Since the IETF is an open and transparent body and in view of the fact that technical recommendations are not directly binding such as laws, a tied accountability regime does not appear necessary.

(3)   WSIS Forum

The WSIS Forum pursues the objective "to review the progress made in the implementation of the WSIS outcomes under the mandates of participating agencies, and to take stock of achievements ... based on reports of WSIS Stakeholders, including those submitted by countries, Action Line Facilitators and other stakeholders".[408] As a consequence, the participants of the WSIS Forum also look into accountability aspects.

In particular, the WSIS 10 High-Level Event in Geneva (2014) published an "Outcome Document"[409] stating for example that "the uses of the ICTs have developed considerably and become a part of everyday life since the second phase of the WSIS in 2005, accelerating social and economic growth, sustainable development, increasing transparency and accountability".

Even if the WSIS Forum as such does not have any accountability mechanisms at its disposal, its stakeholders thoroughly recognize the importance of

---

[405]   See, IETF, The Tao of IETF: A Novice's Guide to the Internet Engineering Task Force, <http://www.ietf.org/about/participate/tao>.

[406]   See IETF, Getting started in the IETF, <http://www.ietf.org/newcomers.html>.

[407]   See IETF, The Internet Standards Process – Revision 3, RFC 2026, <https://tools.ietf.org/html/rfc2026>.

[408]   See <http://www.itu.int/wsis/implementation/2014/forum/>.

[409]   WSIS 10 High-Level Event, Outcome Documents, Geneva 2014, <http://www.itu.int/wsis/implementation/2014/forum/inc/doc/outcome/362828V2E.pdf>.

accountability within the Internet governance framework. By bringing the relevant issues at the table of the Internet Governance Forum, the WSIS Forum contributes to the general improvement of the accountability levels.

(4) Internet Governance Forum

As mentioned,[410] the Internet Governance Forum (IGF) is a multistakeholder platform addressing a wider variety of topics, however, without having decision-making competences. Since the IGF "only" is in a position to submit recommendations and suggestions, the accountability issue is not of major importance and has so far not raised any material concerns.

D. Analysis: Taking Stock and Looking Ahead

The concept of Internet governance is obviously based on the general notion of governance. The (legal) term "governance" can be traced back to the Greek word "*kybernetes*", the "steersman", leading through the Latin word "*gubernator*" to the English notion "governor".[411] Therefore, governance concerns various aspects of steering and governing behavior in different typological extensions (territorial, personal, technological, topical, etc.).

The described regulatory models trying to design a theoretical framework for the development of the Internet governance ecosystem as well as the implementation of the most important substantive governance principles into this framework (such as legitimacy, participation, transparency, accountability) have become more appropriate over time but need further analysis and support.

For example, the detailed information to the developments regarding the substantive principles[412] has shown that transparency and accountability are better dealt with by the Internet governance bodies than participation and (subsequently) legitimacy even if the theoretical models are available. As a consequence, increased emphasis must be put on the realization of multistakeholder models.[413]

---

[410] See above Chapter IV.A.2.5.

[411] *Weber*, 2009, 2.

[412] See above Chapter IV. A to C.

[413] This assessment can also be seen as an answer to the questions raised at the end of Chapter I.

In addition, the processes of international regime formation as well as between sciences and politics need further refinement.[414] The epistemic communities growing in parallel to international organizations can become valuable actors on the way to constructing global collective arrangements.[415] Civil society might have general interests which are not taken into account by the existing international bodies, particularly regarding the implementation of collective values.[416]

Thereby, an appropriate balance between two ideological points of view, represented by the globalists and the sceptics, must be found; the respective positions can be described as follows:[417]

---

[414]   See already *Ruggie*, 1975, 559 et seq.

[415]   *Ruggie*, 1975, 570.

[416]   See also Weber, 2009, 92/93.

[417]   The chart is partly adopted from *Antonova*, 2008, 67/68; see also *Weber*, 2009, 93.

	Globalists	Skeptics
Concepts	– One world, shaped by extensive, intensive and rapid flow of goods/services/data	– Internationalization, not globalization – Regionalization
Power	– Rise of multilateralism – Decline of nation State – Erosion of State sovereignty, autonomy and legitimacy	– Nation State rules – Intergovernmentalism
Culture	– Emergence of global popular culture	– Resurgence of nationalism and national identity
Economy	– Transnational economy – Global informational capitalism	– Development of regional blocs – New imperialism
Inequality	– Growing inequality within and across societies – Erosion of old hierarchies	– Growing North-South divide – Irreconcilable conflicts of interests
Order	– Global civil society – Multilayered global governance – Cosmopolitanism	– International society of States – Political conflicts among States – Communitarianism

Furthermore, the substantive governance principles need to be embedded into an adequate Internet governance "environment". The more "modern" elements including human rights, human security, and human development that have come up during the last five years also require a material broadening of the future Internet governance understanding. Furthermore, the role of transnational organizations that on the one hand regulate and monitor behavior and on the other allocate costs and benefits should be further refined.

A broader understanding of Internet governance could lead to the idea of coining another (wider) notion of its scope such as cybergovernance encompassing additional elements that are important in the online world, for example human integrity (security), culturally-oriented ethics and sustainability. In this perception, cybergovernance can be designed in a way that information and data as well as the related assets and infrastructures are protected in the Internet ecosystem.[418] The next Chapter attempts at revitalizing international legal concepts with the objective of making them fruitful for a better design of the Internet governance ecosystem.

---

[418]   For further details see *Weber*, 2021a, nos. 1 et seq.

V. Revitalization of International Legal Concepts

The conducted analysis of the regulatory models as well as the description of the substantive governance principles has shown that the foundation of Internet regulation in the legal environment is not yet fully satisfactory. Moreover, the recent developments call for an approach that makes the available international normative concepts fruitful for designing Internet governance guidelines. Many concepts are known from other political segments and legal areas but they should gain more importance in the Internet governance context. The subsequently discussed areas are the infrastructural perspectives and the common values of human mankind.

A. Infrastructural Perspectives

The main issues of the infrastructural perspectives are the integrity and stability of cyberspace, the appropriate framework for cybersecurity and the avoidance of Internet fragmentation.

1. Internet Integrity and Stability of Cyberspace

The integrity of cyberspace depends on the proper functioning of the infrastructures' roles without technical interference and (unjustified) governmental intervention. The information technology setting must ensure that data (information) is real, accurate and safeguarded from unauthorized modification. Apart from the technical vulnerability, the aspect of a potential organizational vulnerability also needs to be taken into account.[419] The principle of cyberspace integrity could equally help to overcome the deadlocks occurred in connection with the manifold efforts trying to combat cybersecurity challenges.[420]

The notion of cyberspace integrity gained importance during the last few years since it appears to have a quite broad scope of application (including

---

[419] *Kettemann*, 2020, 26.
[420] For a detailed overview see *Weber*, 2020b, 284 et seq.

human rights and human development).[421] Such a concept can encompass elements of cybersecurity, cyber stability as well as robustness and resilience of the infrastructure. These terms are usually described as follows:[422]

- Cyber stability means that everyone can be reasonably confident in the ability to use the Internet infrastructure in a safe and secure manner; this relatively new term gained importance in connection with the availability and integrity of services and information in the Internet ecosystem.

- Cyber resilience is the ability to provide and maintain an acceptable level of services' rendering and to deliver the envisaged outcome despite adverse cyber events.

Internet integrity allows to effectively and coherently apply the recognized concepts of international law with all its perplexities[423] and to build a normative cyberspace framework that enshrines the described substantive principles (legitimacy, participation, transparency, accountability) in the most suitable manner.[424]

2. Cybersecurity Framework

Cybersecurity is an objective of major importance in the Internet governance context; in substance, it can be seen as a collective action problem. Its definition, however, is still subject to debates, for example in global bodies such as the International Telecommunication Union, the Internet Society or the International Standardisation Organisation.[425]

Manifold threat agents, threat tools and threat types are causing risks to the cross-border infrastructures. Cybersecurity measures should eliminate or at least minimize risks caused by an inappropriate use of international infrastructures. Generally looking, risk is a function of the likelihood of an adverse event, conjoined with the magnitude of harm upon the occurrence of the

---

[421] See *Kettemann*, 2020, 36 et seq.

[422] For a detailed analysis see the *GCSC-Report*, 2019; a recent definition of cybersecurity as well as a cybercrime taxonomy can be found in *Luca Belli*, CyberBRICS: A Multidimensional Approach to Cybersecurity for the BRICS, in: Belli, 2021, 1, 7/8 and 19-22.

[423] See also *Weber*, 2021a, no. 3.

[424] For further details see *Weber*, 2014a, 99 et seq.

[425] See *Weber*, 2020b, 280/81.

adverse event. Precautionary measures are to be taken by governmental and private actors.[426] The technological setting must ensure that data (information) is real, accurate, and safeguarded from unauthorized modification.[427]

As a consequence, from a regulatory perspective, the cybersecurity framework could be established and administered through (i) private institutions with regulatory functions, (ii) hybrid intergovernmental-private arrangements, (iii) distributed regimes of regulators in co-operative schemes, (iv) collective action by transnational networks between officials, or (v) formal international organizations.[428] The implemented measures must be adapted to the prevailing circumstances.

The experience during the last 15 years in the field of cybersecurity has shown that the traditional international law approach operating on the State level through multilateral treaties is hardly able to cope with the challenges of combatting illegal cyber activities. Many expert groups, mainly mandated by the United Nations, published impressive research reports but the attempts of coming to a common understanding on certain principles remained unsuccessful and an implementation of political measures did not take place.[429] Whether the recently launched initiatives with the appointment of two new intergovernmental expert bodies, namely the Open-Ended Working Group (OEWG) and the Group of Governmental Experts (GGE), will be more successful remains to be seen. The respective reports are due towards the end of 2021 but since the underlying UN Resolutions come from different political angles the outcome risks of becoming (slightly) contradictory.[430]

The only exception of a stable legal instrument is the (Budapest) Cybercrime Convention of the Council of Europe (2000)[431] having also been ratified by many (important) non-European countries (for example Argentina, Australia, Canada, Israel, Japan, United States), however, its principles are partly out-

---

[426] Respective measures are particularly addressed in the International Standardisation Organisation's standard 27001 covering "Information technology – Security techniques – Information security management systems – Requirements".

[427] *Weber*, 2021a, no. 7; *Kettemann*, 2020, 26.

[428] *Weber*, 2020b, 307.

[429] For further details, particularly to the five reports of the United Nations Group of Governmental Experts (UNGGE), see *Weber*, 2020b, 285-288, and *Kulesza/Weber*, 2021, 3-5, each with additional references.

[430] See also *Kettemann/Paulus*, 2020, 3, sharing this concern.

[431] Council of Europe, Convention on Cybercrime, ETS no. 185, Budapest, November 2001.

dated since they do not take into consideration the specifics of the Internet.[432] On a regional level, the European Union (EU) implemented the Network and Information Society (NIS) Directive in 2016[433] and the Cybersecurity Act in 2019.[434] These legal instruments promise to improve the integrity and security of the Internet but their geographical scope remains regional.

Assessing the previous transnational attempts of improving cybersecurity it appears to be imperative that the inclusion of a larger number of stakeholders within a new regulatory framework is unavoidable. Such kind of attempt has been undertaken by Microsoft in 2017/18, when it suggested adopting an international treaty to guarantee the peaceful use of cyberspace.[435] The respective proposal to develop a "Digital Geneva Convention" referred to the existing "Treaty on the Non-Proliferation of Nuclear Weapons" and the "Treaty on Chemical Weapons" as examples of international regimes limiting vital threats to human existence. However, the Microsoft proposal was met with skepticisms on the part of many States and its adoption remains uncertain.[436]

In the more business-oriented world, some general security objectives including (i) confidentiality, (ii) integrity, and (iii) availability, also known as the "CIA" triad of the information security industry, have found a certain degree of standardization. The International Organisation for Standardisation (ISO) defines "information security" as the preservation of confidentiality and availability in its "ISO/IEC (International Electrotechnical Commission) 27'000 Family of Information Security Management System Standards".[437]

The presently incoherent patchwork of cybersecurity regulations does not adequately reflect the political needs.[438] So far, the only exception to this pattern is the European Union with its mentioned (directly or indirectly applica-

---

[432] For further details see *Weber*, 2020b, 291-294 with more references.

[433] OJ 2016 L 119/1 of 4 May 2016.

[434] OJ 2019 L 151/15 of 7 June 2019.

[435] Microsoft, Cybersecurity Policy Framework, Geneva, 2018, <https://www.microsoft.com/en-us/cybersecurity/content-hub/cyberscurity-policy-framework>.

[436] *Weber*, 2020b, 307.

[437] See <https://iso.org/standard/54534.html>.

[438] For this reason, the Global Commission on the Stability of Cyberspace has developed substantive principles (so-called "cybernorms") to be adopted by international and national legislators (see *GCSC-Report*, 2019, 6/7).

ble) legal regime consisting of the Network Information Security Directive and the Cybersecurity Act. On the global level, however, further efforts to achieve a better coordinated regulatory framework are required.[439]

3. Avoidance of Fragmentation

The sovereignty principle has its roots in the 16th century. As a term originally "invented" by the philosopher and legal scholar Jean Bodin (1576, "Six Books about the State"), the historical concept goes along with the building-out of nation States.[440] The first (political) document enshrining the sovereignty thinking and prominently reflecting the respective concept is the Westphalian Peace Treaty of 1648. This document encompasses four principles that govern international relations and international law, amongst others the right of each State to monopolize certain exercises of power within its territory and the idea of equality of States including the "one nation one vote" approach related to the decision-making processes in international institutions.[441]

In the meantime, international co-operation[442] and international politics have become important, particularly since the Second World War and the adoption of the UN Charter. The global infrastructures set natural limits to national legislation. Therefore, the traditional sovereignty concept must address (alternative) values involved in a power allocation analysis that could become a new social construct for civil society since profound changes in social and economic patterns challenge States' monopoly on governance.[443] In particular, the following aspects need to be tackled:[444]

– Do States have a shared responsibility based on shared sovereignty to promote and encourage the development of policies?

– Do States have a shared responsibility based on shared sovereignty to ensure fair and equitable allocation of resources?

---

[439] To the most recent challenges see also *DeNardis*, 2020b, 212 et seq.
[440] *Weber*, 2014a, 7.
[441] *Weber*, 2010, 12.
[442] See below Chapter V.B.1.
[443] John H. Jackson, Sovereignty – Modern: A New Approach to an Outdated Concept, 97 American Journal of International Law 2003, 782, 790.
[444] *Weber*, 2010, 16.

–   Do States have a shared responsibility based on shared sovereignty to refrain from influencing the transnational policies related to transboundary information flows?

Governance is changing under conditions of interconnectedness[445] now happening. Power allocation should also include co-operation models and participatory processes enabling civil society to be involved in the technical and legal developments (multistakeholder principle).[446] Such a new concept of co-operative sovereignty leads to a shared responsibility for global resources and to the establishment of standards for interstate co-operation.[447]

Weaknesses in international politics are at least partly responsible for some disarrays in global society.[448] Three phenomena merit to be mentioned: (i) In view of globalization, States can become partly de-constitutionalized by the transfer of governmental functions either to the transnational level or to non-state-actors. (ii) The extraterritorial effects of certain national legislations create a law without sufficient democratic legitimation. (iii) A democratic mandate for transnational governance is widely missing.[449]

Due to various (political) factors, the national governmental flexibility for transnational regulatory frameworks in the network environment[450] has been jeopardized during the last few years since political sensitivities related to sovereignty aspects gained importance. Nation States more frequently claim a right to control the infrastructures and the data flows (for example under the heading of "national security" or "public order" being escape provisions contained in the GATT and the GATS[451]). Thereby, States' interests might often prevail over individual freedoms and human rights values.

Consequently, a certain risk cannot be overlooked that Internet governance will become re-nationalized and the global Internet evolves into the so-called "Splinternet". Some countries (for example Russia) think of creating an independent national Internet. Such a development that leads to fragmentation is

---

445   DeNardis, 2020b, refers in the sub-title of her most recent book to a "world with no switch off".
446   See above Chapter IV.A.2.
447   Weber, 2010, 19.
448   Weber, 2014a, 8.
449   Teubner, 2012, 5.
450   For a general overview see Weyrauch/Winzen, 2020, 1 et seq.
451   For further details see Weber, 2020b, 290.

undesirable. Not surprisingly, in an attempt of avoiding political discussions, ICANN introduced the notion of "Technical Internet Governance" (TIG) being a more neutral language for its business scope. As far as the "lower" technical layer, namely the design or structure of the TIG layer is concerned, the Internet could remain without major fragmentation. In contrast, on the "upper" layer, namely the "use" of the Internet services, a politically-driven fragmentation would be subject to the chosen (governmental) policies.[452]

Apart from the so-called public fragmentation by States relying on a narrower understanding of sovereignty[453] and being interested to increase the own political influence, a certain private fragmentation also occurs, caused by voluntary decisions made by businesses in respect of their own facilities and services as well as made by private intermediaries offering their services.[454]

Looking from a general perspective, any kind of fragmentation would not be future-oriented and have a negative impact on global infrastructures.[455] Moreover, national sovereignty over cross-border communication flows should be replaced by a transnational "popular" (i.e. civil society-based) sovereignty. The respective political concept needs to be strong enough to remove legitimacy and authority over critical aspects of the infrastructure from established governments to non-governmental actors.[456]

As a consequence, in order to avoid fragmentation, the governance functions should remain embedded in horizontal structures creating a decentralized system.[457] In addition, some organized political force would be needed to challenge national sovereignty and stand up for the value of global connectivity as well as for the right of the connected people everywhere to self-govern their online interactions.[458]

B. Realization of Common Values

In view of the fact that the existing multilateral treaties do not appear to sufficiently implement an appropriate Internet framework and to avoid fragmenta-

---

[452] See also *Kleinwächter*, 2021, 6.
[453] See *Hoffmann/Lazanski/Taylor*, 2020, 239 et seq. for the example of China.
[454] *Radu*, 2019, 164, 167/68, 190; see also *Cartwright*, 2020, *passim*.
[455] See also *Voelsen*, 2019, 27/28 and *Voelsen*, 2021, 10.
[456] *Mueller*, 2017, 131.
[457] *Radu*, 2019, 194.
[458] *Mueller*, 2017, 131/32; for a very recent overview see *Haggart/Tusikov/Scholte*, 2021, *passim*.

tion of the global infrastructures, the application of general legal concepts and guidelines becomes necessary. Already fifteen years ago, Antonio Segura-Serrano called on international law to "take a normative stance" in respect of the Internet's future.[459] In this chapter, the call will be taken up with special reference to widely acknowledged normative concepts.

Since decades, "international legal principles" such as customary law or generally accepted behavioral rules (for example acting in good faith) are enshrined in the Statute of the International Court of Justice.[460] But these principles do not (fully) meet the requirements imposed by the Internet environment. Therefore, hereinafter some legal concepts and guidelines particularly suitable for the governing of the Internet ecosystem will be discussed and embedded into a normative order for the Internet.[461]

1. Duty of Co-operation

Co-operation[462] literally means to join forces regarding the realization of a given objective. The duty of co-operation[463] is a concept that has many traces in multilateral declarations as well as in court practice.[464] Art. 1 (1) and (3) of the UN Charter already commit the organization and its members to effective co-operation. Article 11 (1) of the UN Charter refers to the "general principles of co-operation in the maintenance of international peace and security". Chapter IV of the UN Charter is dedicated to "international economic and social co-operation".

The United Nations Covenant on Economic and Social Rights (ICESCR) of 1966 expresses the at least moral commitment for international co-operation in the development context (Art. 2, 3 and 16).[465] The Declaration on the Right to Development of 1966 also calls for international co-operation addressing

---

[459] *Segura-Serrano*, 2006, 271; such kind of "normative stance" is now developed by *Kulesza/ Weber*, 2021, 2 et seq. and 8 seq.

[460] See for example Article 38 of the Statute, <https://www.icj-cij.org/en/statute>.

[461] For a very deep analysis of the normative Internet order see now *Kettemann*, 2020, 233 et seq.; see also *Kerr/Musiani/Pohle*, 2019, 1 et seq.

[462] The term "co-operation" is spelled herein as in most international legal instruments using this term; however, the parallel spelling "cooperation" would be equally correct.

[463] For an analysis of nature and characteristics of the co-operation duty see *Wolfrum*, 2010, paras. 10-12.

[464] For more details see *Weber*, 2021a, nos. 11 et seq.

[465] 993 UNTS 3; for further details see *Kaufmann*, 2018, 318 et seq.

global problems, particularly in its Art. 3.[466] The 2030 Agenda for Sustainable Development encompassing 17 goals requires a higher degree of co-operation.[467] A particular emanation in respect of a co-operation duty is stated in the now fifty years old UN Declaration on Principles of International Law concerning Friendly Relations and Co-operation among States of 1970.[468]

Many other declarations and guidelines include a reference to the co-operation duty. The most prominent example is the Treaty on Principles governing the Activities of States in the Exploration and Use of Outer Space, Including the Moon and Other Celestial Bodies (1967);[469] a similar approach has been chosen by the Law of the Sea (1982).[470] On the regional level, the Helsinki Final Act of the Conference for Security and Co-operation in Europe confirms the need for the co-operation of the participating States in respect of the well-being of people.[471]

In the Golf of Main Case (1984), the International Court of Justice (ICJ) identified a "limited set of norms for ensuring the co-existence and vital co-operation of the members of the international community";[472] these norms exist in parallel to other customary rules being developed as a general standard derived from practice. The ICJ considers the rules related to ensuring "vital co-operation" as central in the context of an equitable solution.[473]

The common global values and the common concerns related to Internet governance call for a coordinated approach in tackling global challenges; co-operation must play a decisive role in the (human and social) development context.[474] A similar approach is chosen in private transactional law; according to Art. 5.1.3 of the UNIDROIT Principles, "each party shall co-operate with the other party when such co-operation may reasonably be expected".[475] In pursuing the objectives of common global values, international law should be transformed from a set of rules preserving the present state of existing relations

---

[466] Adopted by the General Assembly Resolution 41/128 of 4 December 1986.

[467] Adopted by the General Assembly Resolution 70/1 of 25 September 2015.

[468] Adopted by the General Assembly Resolution 2625 (xxv) of 24 October 1970.

[469] 610 UNTS 205.

[470] 1833 UNTS 397.

[471] Final Act of the Conference for Security and Co-operation in Europe, 1 August 1975.

[472] Delimitation of the Maritime Boundary in the Gulf of Maine Area (Canada vs. The United States), 1084 ICJ Rep. 246 (Judgment of 24 February 1984), reprinted in 23 ILM 1197 (1984).

[473] Judgment (supra note 472), no. 111; see also Kettemann, 2020, 90.

[474] See also Wolfrum, 2010, paras. 3/4.

[475] UNIDROIT, Principles of International Commercial Contracts 2016, Rome 2016.

into a regime oriented to fulfil the objective of promoting global social justice.[476] Such appreciation is particularly relevant in the context of an infrastructure (such as the Internet) that must be accessible and usable around the globe.

A "common interests" understanding is not a new idea in the Internet environment[477] but reflects the perception that global infrastructures are part of the "common heritage of mankind". Therefore, the "public core of the Internet" may not any longer be narrowly interpreted as a national interest but rather be seen as a general obligation of States owed to citizens and the international community.[478] By observing the duty of co-operation, States reduce their unilateral impacts as actors of the international community; as a consequence, the traditional approach of assessing inter-state relations as a specific aspect of co-existence moves forward to a concept of joint co-operation between States.[479]

2. Global Public Goods

Global public goods are those goods which benefit humanity as a whole; accordingly these goods should be advantageous to (i) more than one group of countries or geographic regions, to (ii) a broad spectrum of global population, and (iii) to present generations without jeopardizing the ability of future generations to meet their own needs.[480]

From an international law perspective, global public goods theories are not a totally new approach.[481] The idea of a certain "communality" (or "common interest") already lies at the core of two Roman law concepts, namely (i) the "ius cogens" as expression of "compelling" law or of a mandatory norm based on a universal agreement and (ii) "erga omnes" encompassing rights and obligations being owed towards all.[482]

---

[476]   See *Weber*, 2021a, no. 15 with further references.

[477]   See *Kettemann*, 2020, 167 et seq.; see also *Fuchs*, 283 et seq., 301 et seq. and 309 et seq.

[478]   *Kulesza/Weber*, 2021, 6/7; *Kettemann*, 2020, 34.

[479]   See *Weber*, 2021a, nos. 23/24 with further references; for an enhanced co-operation in the cybersecurity context see *Luca Belli*, BRICS Countries to Build Digital Sovereignty, in: Belli, 2021, 271, 277/78.

[480]   *Weber/Menoud*, 2008, 24; *Kaul/Grunberg/Stern*, 1999, 10 et seq.

[481]   See also *Krish*, 2014, 3 et seq. and *Shaffer*, 2012, 675 et seq.

[482]   *Weber/Menoud*, 2008, 24; *Kettemann*, 2020, 33-36.

Further legal concepts do have a similar direction: Global public goods are based on concepts such as "common knowledge" and – as mentioned – "common heritage of mankind".[483] The comparable well-known "public interests" concept is able to peremptorily imposing binding obligations on States.[484] Equally the concept of "critical infrastructures" and their protection is suitable to serve as a point of reference.[485] Consequently, global public goods theories involve a relatively broad understanding that considers political economy implications besides legal aspects.[486]

3. Shared Spaces

The concept of shared spaces to be used by all States in a uniform, non-harmful way is not a new phenomenon in the international community and in international relations. Many global legal areas, constituting a "law on international spaces"[487], exist; already Grotius in the seventeenth century explained the law of all nations as the law "derived from nature, the common mother of us all, and whose sway extends over those who rule nations".[488] In particular, the feature common to all international spaces encompasses the obligation of peaceful use of resources and the principle of equal rights of all States.[489]

Examples can be mainly found in air and space law as well as in laws of the sea. (i) The Treaty of Principles Governing the Activities of States in the Exploration and Use of Outer Space, Including the Moon and Other Celestial Bodies of 1976[490] has the objective that all participating States (i) submit their outer space activities to international law, as well as (ii) implement the principles of non-discrimination and of non-appropriation by any claim of sovereignty. The most important rules for the maritime area (i.e. oceans) as contained in the Convention on the High Seas (1958)[491] and in the Convention on the Law of the

---

[483] *Kulesza/Weber*, 2017, 81/82; the Report of the UN Secretary-General's Roadmap for Digital Cooperation, June 2020, 8, also refers to "digital public goods" <https://www.un.org/en/content/digital-cooperation-roadmap/>.

[484] *Weber*, 2020b, 304.

[485] See also *Weber/Menoud*, 2008, 25-27; *Stoll*, 2008, 116 et seq.; *Kulesza/Weber*, 2017, 82 et seq.

[486] For further details to public global goods see *Weber*, 2021b, Chapter II.2.

[487] This term was introduced by *Kish*, 1973 (title of the book).

[488] *Grotius*, 1916, 5.

[489] For a detailed analysis of this concept see *Weber*, 2021b, Chapter II.3 with further references.

[490] 610 UNTS 205.

[491] 450 UNTS 11.

Sea (1982)[492] concern (i) the freedom of the seas' principle and (ii) the regulation of the common space for the economic exploitation of the oceans leading to a wider and multifaceted co-operation.[493]

Even if a concise and general assessment cannot be derived from the mentioned and also from other areas of international law, the basic normative principles are suitable to be made fruitful in the context of Internet governance. Nation States should closely co-operate in a continuing effort to arrive at an operable consensus that takes into consideration global interoperability, network stability, reliable access and cybersecurity measures.[494]

4. Due Diligence

Due diligence is a general legal concept which is applicable in many different fields. Due diligence can be qualified as a behavioral rule; the contents concern the acting with "due care" in the exercise of given functions. The concept of due diligence is an expression of informed decision-making processes; it corresponds to the German notion of "Sorgfaltspflicht" and the French notion of "vigilance".[495]

The due diligence concept appears as a shared element of treaty-based regimes, but it has a very broad scope of application also extending to private actors as can be seen from the OECD Due Diligence Guidance.[496] Therefore, the concept appears to be now embedded in the international discourse and in the practices of stakeholders across the spectrum.[497]

The concept of due diligence has mainly become important in environmental matters. Particularly, the concept is well established in connection with the guidance of preventing transboundary harm.[498] By analogy, the due diligence standards can also be made fruitful in the context of Internet governance since the avoidance of "transboundary harm" corresponds to the omission of

---

[492]   1833 UNTS 397.

[493]   See *Weber*, 2014a, 20.

[494]   See also *Heintschel von Heinegg*, 2013, 134 et seq.

[495]   For further details to the term "due diligence" see *Kaufmann*, 2020, 77 et seq. and *Rolf H. Weber/Rainer Baisch*, Liability of Parent Companies for Human Rights Violations of Subsidiaries, European Business Law Review 27/5 (2016), 669, 685 et seq.

[496]   OECD, Guidance on Due Diligence, Paris 2018.

[497]   *Smit/Bright*, 2020, 51 et seq.

[498]   See *Smit/Bright*, 2020, 51 et seq. with reference to the EU Study on Due Diligence Requirements of April 2020; *Kettemann*, 2020, 95/96 and 97-101; *Kulesza*, 2016, 205 et seq.

all activities that could potentially disrupt communications channels within a State territory.[499] Similarly, the same assessment is relevant for community standards related to good practices within specific Internet sectors (e.g. root zone operation, IXP operation, DMS and TLD management).[500]

Looking at the newest international developments, the concept of due diligence has turned out to be a widely acknowledged guideline in cross-border relations, for example equally as a principle in the context of cyber operations foreseen in the Tallinn Manual 2.0.[501] Therefore, due diligence merits achieving higher attention also in the Internet governance environment; governments should closely co-operate in a continuing effort to arrive at an operable consensus that pursues cyber-related global interoperability.[502]

5.   State Responsibility

The legal principle of State responsibility constitutes a general normative concept that has a (partial) hard law quality exceeding the level of generally accepted soft law standards and that is applicable in addition to all other specified international legal norms imposing obligations upon States.[503] If a transboundary obligation of a State (be it an obligation of conduct or one of result) is breached, the consequences provided for in the law of State responsibility entail.

The main normative document in this field was developed by the International Law Commission (ILC) in long-lasting efforts; the so-called Draft Articles on Responsibility of States for Internationally Wrongful Acts of 2001 have been adopted by the UN General Assembly Resolution 56/83 and became part of the customary law also applied by the International Court of Justice.[504] The ILC based its work on two fundamental assumptions: (i) a breach of an inter-

---

[499]   Kulesza, 2016, 276 et seq. and 288 et seq. with further references.

[500]   Kulesza/Weber, 2017, 82 et seq.

[501]   Tallinn Manual 2.0 on the International Law Applicable to Cyber Operations, 2017; due diligence will remain an important principle in the version Tallinn Manual 3.0 as now prepared.

[502]   See also Weber, 2021b, Chapter II.4; to the due diligence principle in other legal areas see Kettemann, 2020, 97-101.

[503]   Kulesza, 2016, 115 et seq.

[504]   Draft Articles on Responsibility of States for International Wrongful Acts, ILC Report, 2001, UN Doc. A/56/10.

national obligation existing as a so-called primary norm can lead to a responsibility either based on a specific "sanction" or on a general international principle. (ii) An international wrongful act causes a State responsibility.[505]

The responsibility principle is linked to the already mentioned due diligence requirement implying a duty of States to act with proper care in preventing a violation of international law.[506] By analogy, a due diligence standard for Internet integrity with shared responsibility could equally build an entry point for State responsibility in respect of an omission (for example a disruption of communication channels) resulting in transboundary harm.[507]

6. Further Concepts

In its recent Report on Cyberstability, published in November 2019 at the occasion of the yearly IGF (Berlin), the Global Commission on the Stability of Cyberspace (GCSC) presented three additional principles having a legal notion:

> – The requirement of "restraint" imposes on State and non-state actors the behavioral rule to act in accordance with general principles of international peace and security; thereby, harmful acts that could undermine the resilience and stability of cyberspace can be avoided.[508]
>
> – The requirement to "act principle" contains the duty to take affirmative action for preserving the stability of cyberspace; State and non-state actors should take care that inadvertently escalating tensions or increasing instability are avoided.[509]
>
> – Furthermore, human rights should play a more important role in connection with the availability and integrity of networks and infrastructures allowing the cross-border flow of information and data.[510]

---

[505] For further details see *Kulesza*, 2016, 149 et seq.; *Kurbalija*, 2016, 318 et seq.
[506] See above Chapter V.B.4.
[507] *Weber* 2021b, Chapter II.4; *Kulesza*, 2016, 253 et seq.; *Kurbalija*, 2016, 323.
[508] *GCSC-Report*, 2019, 18.
[509] *GCSC-Report*, 2019, 19.
[510] *GCSC-Report*, 2019, 19.

The mentioned concepts developed by the GCSC in respect of cyberspace stability, complemented by eight specific norms,[511] can equally play a role in the context of Internet governance since their contents concern the environment of a global infrastructure in general.

C. Concluding Remarks

As shown in this Chapter, international legal concepts become increasingly important in the Internet governance environment. Due to the lack of sufficient governmental instruments such as multilateral treaties, these normative guidelines implementing a multistakeholder approach need to be further developed and refined. The so far (incoherent) patchwork of Internet integrity rules does not meet the requirements of the given political and societal needs.

The governance of the Internet with its cosmopolitan structures constitutes an issue of global common concern. The protection of Internet integrity is necessary for safeguarding its functioning in the interest of States and civil society. Mutual co-operative efforts in solving occurring problems and in developing new cross-border understandings help to transform the present situation into a better and improved ecosystem guaranteeing appropriate Internet governance policies.

---

[511] GCSC-*Report*, 2019, 21/22.

VI. Outlook

At the time of the two WSIS Summits (2003/05), Internet governance was often seen as a mainly technical issue with some political implications. The domain name system, the protocols and exchange points as well as the potential barriers for innovation were at the core of the debates, partly combined with aspects of censorship and protectionism. Now, the equation appears to have reversed: Internet governance has become a mainly political issue with a technical component.[512] In a similar way, Delvenne/Parotte use the following equation: technology "has politics" and technology "as politics".[513]

From a substantive perspective this impression of a new Internet governance understanding is mirrored in the ongoing developments: presently, the range of topics is much broader than 15 years ago since many themes with political impacts (for example human rights and sustainable development which cannot easily be mirrored in the technical Internet architecture[514]) attract higher attention. Not surprisingly, the terminology also changed with the move from Internet governance to cybergovernance.[515] The basic governance objectives, however, remain the same: the Internet ecosystem should contribute (i) to overcoming fragmentation and realizing multistakeholderism as well as (ii) to supporting common values and enhanced co-operation.

Overcoming fragmentation and realizing multistakeholderism

Due to the shift into the political arena and the stronger position of some countries (often with autocratic governments not based on traditional Western democracy concepts) in the Internet ecosystem, disruptions in respect of global Internet governance have occurred.[516] Such a development contradicts the common values' and the common interests' perceptions. Moreover, given the complex Internet environment, multidimensional policy spaces need to be developed allowing the creation of knowledge and innovation.[517] In addition,

---

[512] *Kleinwächter/Kettemann/Senges/Schweiger*, 2020, 3.
[513] *Delvenne/Parotte*, 2019, 64 (in title of article).
[514] See *Mueller/Badiei*, 2019, 61 et seq.
[515] *Weber*, 2021a, nos. 1 et seq.
[516] See also *DeNardis*, 2020b, 188 et seq.
[517] See *Levinson*, 2020, 278.

an interdisciplinary understanding encompassing technologies and social sciences should prevail in the design of Internet governance and in the dissemination of policies' results to all members of civil society.[518]

Over the last few years, new initiatives have been started by the United Nations. The manifold discussion lines were gathered by and channeled through the UN High-Level Panel on Digital Cooperation (HLP).[519] The HLP Final Report of 2019 presented five groups of recommendations[520] and the deliberations have continued since the Report's publication in the form of virtual "Roundtables" aiming at the preparation of "Opinion Papers" that could lead to the adoption of a "Global Commitment on Digital Cooperation".[521] Additionally, in June 2020, the UN Secretary-General published a "Roadmap for Digital Cooperation".[522] The primary objective of these discussion rounds and documents consists in the attempt of laying the foundation for an increasingly inclusive and effective Internet Governance Forum by 2025 (at the occasion of its 20th anniversary), namely for a more dynamic "IGF+".[523]

However, the manifold available reports as well as the deliberations during the annual Internet Governance Forum (IGF) as market place for information and ideas around Internet-related technical and political issues cannot hide the fact that the available mechanisms still have some weaknesses. The pragmatic approach based on the assumption that decisions should not be made inside, but outside the IGF, does not solve the prevailing problem: no procedure is in place which converts the "theoretical ideas" into "practical negotiations", i.e. there is no "landing place" for multistakeholder knowledge and wisdom.[524]

Numerous multistakeholder and interdisciplinary projects and initiatives have been launched during the last few years, for example the Contract for the Web (Tim Berners-Lee), the Paris Call for Trust and Security, the Global Commission on the Stability of Cyberspace, the Internet & Jurisdiction Policy Network (Paris) having published three "Toolkits" (Cross-Border Access to Electronic Evidence, Cross-Border Content Moderation, DNS Level Action to Address

---

[518] For a more detailed analysis of the different interdisciplinary approaches see *Epstein/Katzenbach/Musiani*, 2015, 3 et seq.

[519] See <https://digitalcooperation.org/>.

[520] See <https://www.giplatform.org/resources/hlp-report>.

[521] *Kettemann/Paulus*, 2020, 2.

[522] See Report of the UN Secretary-General's Roadmap for Digital Cooperation, June 2020, <https://www.un.org/en/content/digital-cooperation-roadmap/>.

[523] See also *Kettemann/Paulus*, 2020, 2.

[524] *Kleinwächter/Kettemann/Senges/Schweiger*, 2020, 3.

Abuses) in March 2021, the Tech Accord (Microsoft), the Global Forum on Cyber Expertise, etc. These groups should attempt at joining forces with their valuable activities in order to overcome national approaches that cause a substantial risk an Internet fragmentation.[525]

Such national approaches prioritizing country-specific interests have been recently pursued by several governments, for example by the United States mainly in the context of political assessments or by China with the "Global Initiative on Data Security" of 8 September 2020[526] and with the "Wuzhen Plan" of Foreign Minister Wang Yi presented prior to the World Internet Conference (WIC, Wuzhen) of November 2020.[527] Furthermore, a certain risk exists that State power is internationalized through private actors (such as big social media or telecom operators).[528] Such national initiatives contradict the inherent value of Internet governance that touches upon aspects which have a "common interest" character being a well-known concept in transnational law.[529]

In general, the number of global challenges is increasing. Apart from human rights and human security, development issues and more recently (environmental) sustainability gain importance. Specifically, the sustainability topic has received much attention during the (online) IGF 2020; as a consequence, the IGF Secretariat has now implemented a "Policy Network" as well as a new intersessional "working team" dealing with the interplay between digitalization processes and environment.[530] This topic is (rightly) placed higher on the Internet governance global agenda and will contribute to the overall goal of protecting the environment and planetary health as well as promoting forward-looking sustainability objectives.

---

[525]   See above Chapter V.A.3.

[526]   See <https://www.fmprc.gov.cn/mfa_eng/zxxx_662805/t1812951.shtml>.

[527]   See <https://www.wuzhenwic.org>. The main problem consists in the lack of important Internet governance elements such as multistakeholderism and bottom-up policies which do not seem to be relevant in the Chinese perception; possibly this fact is due to the general Chinese appreciation that is more based on network governance than on the "traditional" Internet governance (see *Chin*, 2020, 134 et seq.).

[528]   *Cartwright*, 2020, *passim*.

[529]   See also *Kettemann*, 2014, 167 et seq.

[530]   See   <https://www.intgovforum.org/multilingual/content/policy-network-on-environment-and-digitalisation-pne>.

Supporting common values and enhanced co-operation

As mentioned, the substantive contents of the "common interest" must be based on widely accepted norms and values which are the foundation for responsible behavior and activities (i.e. co-operation between States, compliance with human rights and privacy, protection of critical infrastructures, coordination of preventive measures against network misuses, etc.).[531] Most importantly, such norms and values that mirror quality elements should enable the creation of trust not only among States,[532] but equally among States and private actors being also – as mentioned – "keepers of international law".[533] Such an approach could be strengthened by the implementation of human rights, social and ethical impact assessments.[534]

This aspect of (digital) trust[535] has been compared by Internet governance experts with the picture of a "spaghetti-ball" showing that the individual issues are like "single spaghettis" with two ends, namely one multistakeholder and one multilateral, connected by "cheese" and "tomato sauce" that are suitable to build a common trustworthy philosophy regarding the appropriate and properly designed application of international legal concepts.[536] By pursuing this path the chances increase that the Internet will not be "owned" by a few powerful entities but by all concerned actors.[537]

Based on the assessed policy parameters for Internet rule-making and the guiding principles of a normative online order, the core of the concept of Internet governance must be embedded into (i) internationalized policy structures, (ii) a procedural regime relying on multilayer models and multistakeholder participation, (iii) appropriate substantive principles as well as (iv) the functional dimensions of a cosmopolitan constitutional framework.[538] Thereby,

---

[531] A visual overview has insofar been given by *Kettemann/Paulus*, 2020, 1.

[532] See also *Levinson*, 2020, 272.

[533] *Butler*, 2020, 189.

[534] *Mantelero*, 2018, 754 et seq.

[535] Digital trust is also addressed as a relevant objective in the UN Secretary-General's Roadmap for Digital Cooperation (supra note 522), 19/20. Obviously, digital trust equally concerns the protection of individuals against (far-reaching State) surveillance having become an intensively discussed (but in this book not to be deepened) topic since the Snowden revelations (for further details see *Zuboff*, 2019, *passim*).

[536] This picture was recently used by *Kleinwächter/Kettemann/Senges/Schweiger*, 2020, 4.

[537] The risk that the Internet is "owned" by a few powerful actors is described in detail by *Lanier*, 2013, *passim*.

[538] *Weber*, 2014a, 149.

no compromise appears to be justified with regard to fundamental legal principles such as the rule of law, digital human rights,[539] and democracy. Obviously, these principles are subject to interpretation[540] but their core (*nucleus*) cannot be negotiable in the online world.

As a consequence, more elements of enhanced co-operation should be implemented in order to overcome a "silo-approach" that addresses single solutions; rather, a "holistic approach" is needed that makes the realities of a fast-changing environment in an interconnected world compatible with the implementation of the appropriate political strategies.[541] Such an approach also calls for more co-regulation in different forms that enables public as well as private actors to join legislative forces.[542] Thereby, the governance model could consist of three modes, namely the multilateral, the multistakeholder and the emergent level; these three modes appear to be desirable for realizing a governance of commons.[543]

Based on these premises, more dynamic initiatives supporting cross-border connectivity and digital inclusion[544] have a fair chance to lead to a convincing global architecture for Internet governance. In the current "Internet of Everything" being a "World with No Switch Off", as recently framed by Laura DeNardis,[545] it is imperative to establish generally acknowledged concepts and standards of international law allowing the whole civil society to contribute to the Internet governance ecosystem.

---

[539] See also the UN Secretary-General's Roadmap for Digital Cooperation (supra note 522), 14 et seq.

[540] DeNardis, 2020b, 163, uses the term "oxymoron" in respect of the notion of "Internet freedom"; however, such a qualification would definitely not be appropriate in respect of the "rule of law" and "human rights".

[541] *Kleinwächter/Kettemann/Senges/Schweiger*, 2020, 4.

[542] For an extensive analysis of the co-regulation approach in the information society see the study of *Spindler/Thorun*, 2016, 1 et seq.; to the ongoing co-regulation discussions see recently *Marsden*, 2020, 52/53, and *Weber*, 2021b, Chapter III.2.

[543] See *Lazanski*, 2019, 362 et seq.

[544] See also the UN Secretary General's Roadmap for Digital Cooperation (supra note 522), 5-7 and 10/11.

[545] DeNardis, 2020b; the text cites a part of the title of the book.

Assuming the Point of No Return

Despite some challenges and problems in the future embodiment of enhanced co-operation the Internet governance concept appears to be at the *point of no return*. Looking at the developments since the two WSIS Summits it can hardly be imagined that the IGF will not continue after 2025. Therefore, the following vision may be expressed at this stage: Internet governance should become the "narrative" for the conceptual design of policies and legal norms making cyberspace a livable and trustworthy place for civil society. In other words, the forward-looking paths should be structured in a comprehensible manner through a narrative that follows the common values perceptions of the concerned civil society.

Based on such a concept, the discussed *international legal concepts*[546] should become more apparent and be implemented in the Internet governance ecosystem. In the interest of all involved actors (governments, businesses, civil society, etc.) Internet governance "participants" would thereby contribute to making *international law more visible*.

---

[546]   See above Chapter V.